T0313248

STUDIES ON INDUSTRIAL PRODUCTIVITY:
SELECTED WORKS

Volume 6

A STUDY OF INNOVATIVE BEHAVIOR IN HIGH TECHNOLOGY PRODUCT DEVELOPMENT ORGANIZATIONS

A STUDY OF
INNOVATIVE BEHAVIOR
IN HIGH TECHNOLOGY PRODUCT
DEVELOPMENT ORGANIZATIONS

MARK ANTHONY ROBBEN

Routledge
Taylor & Francis Group

LONDON AND NEW YORK

First published in 1999 by Garland Publishing Inc.

This edition first published in 2019
by Routledge
2 Park Square, Milton Park, Abingdon, Oxon OX14 4RN

and by Routledge
711 Third Avenue, New York, NY 10017

Routledge is an imprint of the Taylor & Francis Group, an informa business

© 1999 Mark Anthony Robben

British Library Cataloguing in Publication Data
A catalogue record for this book is available from the British Library

ISBN: 978-1-138-61548-9 (Set)
ISBN: 978-0-429-44077-9 (Set) (ebk)
ISBN: 978-1-138-32597-5 (Volume 6) (hbk)
ISBN: 978-0-429-45005-1 (Volume 6) (ebk)

Publisher's Note
The publisher has gone to great lengths to ensure the quality of this reprint but points out that some imperfections in the original copies may be apparent.

Disclaimer
The publisher has made every effort to trace copyright holders and would welcome correspondence from those they have been unable to trace.

A STUDY OF INNOVATIVE BEHAVIOR IN HIGH TECHNOLOGY PRODUCT DEVELOPMENT ORGANIZATIONS

MARK ANTHONY ROBBEN

GARLAND PUBLISHING, INC.
A MEMBER OF THE TAYLOR & FRANCIS GROUP
NEW YORK & LONDON / 1999

Published in 1999 by
Garland Publishing Inc.
a Member of the Taylor & Francis Group
19 Union Square West
New York, NY 10003

10   9   8   7   6   5   4   3   2   1

Library of Congress Cataloging-in-Publication Data

Robben, Mark Anthony.
    A study of innovative behavior : in high technology product
development organizations / Mark Anthony Robben.
        p.   cm. — (Garland studies on industrial productivity)
    Includes bibliographical references and index.
    ISBN 0-8153-3489-3 (alk. paper)
    1. Creative ability in business.   2. Technological innovations.
3. High technology industries.   I. Title.   II. Series.
HD53.R59   1999
658.5'14—dc21   99-15565
                                                              CIP

Printed on acid-free, 250-year-life paper
Manufactured in the United States of America

To my daughters
Amy, Stacey, and Megan

Contents

Preface

This study integrates several streams of research on the antecedents of innovation to test a model of individual innovative behavior in a high technology product development organization. The world we live in today is a globally competitive environment of rapidly changing technologies. Organizations must harness the innovative potential of their employees to create better and novel ways to solve old and new problems or risk becoming extinct. Innovative organizations can gain a competitive advantage over their less innovative competition through better products, faster product development times and lower priced products.

It was hypothesized that individual problem solving style, leadership, climate for innovation, and leader expectations affect innovative behavior in high technology product development organizations. Six null hypotheses were used to test the research question. Kirton's (1976) Adaption-Innovation theory was used to define and measure individual problem solving style. The three sub-factors that make up the total KAI score were evaluated separately. The theory developed by Graen and Cashman (1975) and Graen, Novak and Scandura (1987) on leader-member exchange was used to define and measure the quality of the leader-member exchange between supervisor and subordinate. Role expectation theory was based on an article by Livingston, (1969) and work by Scott and Bruce (1994). The theory for work climate and innovative behavior was taken largely from the work by Siegel and Kaemmer, (1978) and Abey and Dickerson, (1983).

The research sample for this research was a group of 81 Engineers, Designers, and Lab Technicians employed in an Engineering Department responsible for the development high technology products. The base sample in this research was evaluated using structural equation modeling techniques and multiple linear regression. The base sample was divided into the four sub groups of Product Engineers, Application Engineers, Lab Technicians, and Product Designers. An additional subgroup was obtained from Management Engineers who filled out subordinate survey packages. The research data from each subgroup was analyzed using multiple linear regression to identify the determinants of individual innovative behavior for each subgroup. Each of the six null hypotheses were rejected for at least one of the subgroup. The determinants of individual innovative behavior varied greatly for each of the five subgroups.

In this research some interesting results were obtained with the Kirton Adaption-Innovation Inventory (KAI). The KAI score is the summation of the three sub-factors, sufficiency versus proliferation of originality, preference for efficiency, and rule/group conformity. In previous use of the KAI in the general population respondents scored consistently high or low in each of the three KAI sub-groups. In this study, innovative people in the high technology product development organization did not follow this general population trend. Unlike previous KAI studies the innovative people indicated a preference for efficiency as defined by Kirton. This makes intuitive sense in that to be innovative in a complex high technology environment an individual must have a preference toward efficiency to keep the complex information organized. As the complexity of information required in a high technology product development organization increases so must the complexity of innovative people increase.

Acknowledgments

There are a number of people whom this researcher is very grateful to for their assistance and guidance. First, Dr. William Snow for his guidance and encouragement throughout the process. Second, Dr. Moshe Levin and Dr. Randy Hilton for their valuable comments and input. Third, Dr. Werner Wothke, the president of SmallWaters Corporation, which publishes Amos, for his assistance with structural equation modeling.

Nova Southeastern University deserves a special thanks for creating a DBA program around students who are often employed full time. Five days a week this researcher experiences real world management and innovation challenges at a full time job. The Nova program created an opportunity to combine real world experience with academic knowledge and earn a doctorate degree by studying weekends, evenings, and vacations.

This researcher is deeply indebted to XYZ Company for believing in this research and making their Engineering personnel available for this research. Real world academic research would not exist if it were not for such forward looking companies. Companies often get caught up in their own internal politics and competitiveness and will not give academic research a fair chance. This researcher experienced this phenomenon first hand after working with a large computer manufacture for about one year on this innovation research.

Last, but not least I would like to thank my daughters, Amy, Stacey, and Megan, for enduring this long research project. Many opportunities to mountain-bike, hike, camp, and ski together have been postponed.

Tables and Figures

CHAPTER 1

Introduction

BACKGROUND

Today, we live in a globally competitive world of rapidly changing technologies. Those organizations that are unable to come up with better and novel ways to solve old and new problems may soon become extinct. Organizations that are successful in bringing out the innovative potential of their personnel will gain a competitive advantage over their less innovative competitors in this rapidly changing environment by generating new and innovative products.

Innovation plays a major role in the long term survival of organizations (Ancona & Caldwell, 1987). According to Wren, D. A. (1994), Peter Drucker views organizations as being in a constant state of creation, growth, stagnation, and decline and it is an organization's ability to innovate that keeps it from failing. Innovative organizations also respond more readily to change than adaptive organizations (Foxall, Gordon & Payne, Adrain, 1989). Innovation is a subset of a construct of organizational change. Organizational change can include innovation, but not all organizational change is innovation (Woodman, Sawyer, & Griffin, 1993).

Managing for innovation must be different from the managing of ongoing, established operations where the desire or expectation of change is to a much smaller degree. The less structured process of innovation is at odds with the more structured administrative process of increased efficiency in established operations. Structures and practices that work well in established operations tend to be at odds with the innovative process (Kanter, 1988).

The innovation process tends to have four distinctive characteristics. The characteristics are similar for technological or administrative and for products, processes or systems (Kanter, 1988). The first characteristic given by Kanter is that the innovation process is uncertain. The timing of an innovation or the opportunity to innovate can be unpredictable. Innovations often involve unknown territory so accurately forecasting results or forecasts is difficult. Quinn (1979) wrote that "Progress on a new innovation . . . comes in spurts among unforeseen delays and setbacks . . . in the essential chaos of development." Innovative results are highly uncertain and actual cost are often unanticipated (Kanter, 1988).

The second characteristic given by Kanter is that the innovation process is knowledge-intensive. The innovation process relies on individual human intelligence and creativity and involves "interactive learning" (Quinn, 1985). New knowledge and new experiences are generated quickly in a short amount of time. The learning curve is steep during the innovative process. Turnover during the innovative process can be devastating because knowledge and experience can be lost before it is transferred to others in the organization (Kanter, 1988).

The third characteristic given by Kanter is that the innovation process is controversial. Innovative ideas often involve alternative solutions to problems and those with vested interest in one particular solution may feel threatened. The individual being threatened by innovation could be anyone from a manager of a department that would be down sized, to a salesman that may lose commissions on current products. The major cause for the failure of corporate New Venture Departments is "political" problems (Fast, 1979).

The fourth characteristic given by Kanter is that the innovation process crosses boundaries. The success of most innovative ideas involve several departments because one department does not have all that is necessary to make the innovative idea a success. Many innovative ideas are interdisciplinary or interfunctional and require the combination of existing departments or boundaries. New innovations may require that other departments in an organization change their behavior to support the new innovation. The new innovation may require that other departments generate other innovative ideas to support the primary innovation (Kanter, 1988).

Innovation is a process that is uncertain, fragile, political, and imperialistic. Innovation is most likely to thrive in an organization that allows flexibility, quick action and intensive care, coalition formation, and connectedness (Kanter, 1988). There must be flexibility in the organization structure and individual job descriptions to allow individuals to "do what it takes" to move innovative ideas forward.

There are several kinds of innovations. Product innovations are more likely to occur in organizations that are new to the market and process innovations are more likely to occur in established organizations. It is also found that product innovations are more common in the early stages of a product and process innovations are more likely to take place in later stages of a product (Abernathy & Utterback, 1978). It is also found that technological innovations are more likely when resources are abundant and administrative innovations are more likely when resources are scarce (Kimberly, 1981). Incremental change type innovations are more likely in organizations that are more rigid and centralized while more revolutionary innovations are more likely in organizations that are less rigid and decentralized (Cohn & Turyn, 1984).

Researchers exploring innovation have recognized that the generation of ideas is only one stage of a multistage process. Kanter (1988) listed four major innovation tasks, which correspond to the stages of the innovation process. The tasks listed by Kanter (1988) are:

(a) idea generation and activation of the drivers of the innovation (the "entrepreneurs" or "innovators");
(b) coalition building and acquisition of the power necessary to move the idea into reality;
(c) idea realization and innovation production, turning the idea into a model—a product or plan or prototype that can be used;
(d) transfer or diffusion, the spreading of the model—the commercialization of the product, the adoption of the idea.

Individuals can be involved in various combinations of the innovation stages at the same time, since innovation is characterized by discontinuous activities rather than discrete, sequential stages (Schroeder, Van de Ven, Scudder, & Polley, 1989). The various stages of the innovation process require different activities and different individual behaviors for each stage (Scott & Bruce, 1994).

The first task in the innovation process begins with idea generation and innovation activation. An innovative individual starts the innovative process with problem recognition and the generation of ideas or solutions, either novel or adopted that depart from the organization's established routines or systems (Kanter, 1988). The innovative idea will not survive unless someone recognizes the potential of the idea and exerts the energy necessary to raise the idea over the threshold of consciousness. The goal of innovation management is to get individuals to come up with innovative ideas and then get individuals to appreciate and pay attention to new ideas, needs and opportunities (Kanter, 1988).

The second task in the innovation process is coalition building. Previous studies of the innovation process have shown the importance of backers and supporters in high places, to the success of innovation (Quinn, 1979; Maidique, 1980). An innovative individual or group of individuals must seek sponsorship for the innovative idea to gain support. It is important that upper management be sold on the innovative idea to insure the resources required for proper development are allocated.

The third task in the innovation process is idea realization and innovation production. This task involves putting together a working team to transform the innovative idea into a working and tangible object that can be handed off to others (Kanter, 1988). Through an innovative individual "a prototype or model of the innovation is produced that can be touched or experienced, that can now be diffused, mass-produced, turned to productive use, or institutionalized" (Kanter, 1988).

The third task in the innovation process is transfer and diffusion. In this process the innovative idea will be transferred to those who will use the innovative idea in ongoing organizational practice and projects (Kanter, 1988). An innovative individual must insure that the innovative idea is transferred properly and another innovative individual must take the innovative idea and implement into current practices or projects. The four tasks, each with different activities, require individuals with innovative behavior to carry them out (Scott & Bruce, 1994).

PURPOSE OF STUDY

The purpose of this research was to study the determinants of individual innovative behavior in a high technology product development organization. There has been limited attention given to innovation at the individual level (West & Farr, 1989). Scott and Bruce (1994) made a study that integrated several independent streams of research on the antecedents of creativity, innovation, and organizational climate in a research and development organization. This research extends the Scott and Bruce study (1994) from a research and development environment to a high technology organization responsible for product development.

High technology product development organizations are under continuous pressure to generate new products that will sell at a profit. This means the products must get to the market quickly, be better than the competition, and be sold at an acceptable cost. These pressures are different from strictly research and development organizations where the pace can be much slower. The determinants of individual innovative behavior in the quick pace high technology product development organizations may be quite different from research and development organizations. This research investigates determinants of individual innovative behavior in a high technology product development organization and compares these results with other research, such as the Scott and Bruce (1994) study, in a research and development organization.

This research investigated the relationship between several factors known to influence individual innovative behavior in research and development organizations in a high technology organization involved in product development. Previous research has indicated a positive relationship between individual innovative behavior and several factors. These factors are problem solving style, leadership, leader expectations and perception of the work climate. Established questionnaires was used to measure individual problem solving style, leadership, leader expectations, and perception of work climate. The level of individual innovative behavior was measured using methods established by Scott and Bruce (1994). Structural equation modeling was used to quantify and establish relationships between the factors and individual innovative behavior.

SIGNIFICANCE OF STUDY

The foundation of innovation is ideas and it is the individual people in an organization who "develop, carry, react to, and modify ideas" (Van de Ven, 1986). Innovative behavior has a central role in the long-term survival of organizations (Anacona & Caldwell, 1987). The study of what promotes individual innovative behavior in organizations is critical for a better understanding of how organizations can manage the level of innovative behavior in their organizations (Scott & Bruce, 1994).

Management can have a positive impact on individual innovative behavior in their organizations. A thorough knowledge of the relationships between individual innovative behavior and those factors known to influence individual innovative behavior is crucial. This research investigated the factors known to influence innovative behavior in a research and development organization in a high technology product development organization. The results of this research can be used to better understand the influence of problem solving style, leadership, leader expectations, and positive perception of work climate on individual innovative behavior in high technology product development organizations.

High technology product development organizations can use the information generated from this research to better manage the level of innovative behavior in their organization. The level of individual innovative behavior in a particular group can be managed by controlling factors that are known to influence individual innovative behavior. One of the possibilities is to modify the problem solving style make-up of a group by removing and/or adding members with preferred problem solving style. The adaptive versus innovative level of problem solving style for a product development group can be adjusted to optimal levels once the best level is understood.

Information gained from this research can help management to understand the relationship between the quality of leadership and innovative behavior. With this new information, management can better organize leadership training to improve innovative behavior in their organizations. This research also investigated the relationship between individual innovative behavior and individual perceptions of the work climate. A better understanding of the relationship between individual innovative behavior and individual perception of work climate can be used by management to improve work climate such that individual innovative behavior is increased.

The information generated from this research can be used by high technology product development organizations to increase innovative behavior. Organizations that are able to manage the level of individual innovative behavior in various work groups within their organization will more effectively utilize their innovative talent and increase innovative idea generation within their organization.

THEORY/ASPECT OF THEORY BEING TESTED

This research brings together several theories related to individual innovative behavior. In previous studies these theories were found to have an influence on individual innovative behavior in organizations. In this research four theories were used to define and measure independent variables expected to influence individual innovative behavior. Kirton's (1976) Adaption-Innovation theory is used to define and measure individual problem solving style. The theory developed by Graen and Cashman (1975) and Graen, Novak and Scandura (1987) on leader-member exchange is used to define and measure the quality of the leader-member exchange between supervisors and subordinates. Role expectation theory is based on an article by Livingston, (1969) titled "Pygmalion in Management." The theory for work climate and innovative behavior was taken largely from the work by Siegel and Kaemmerer, (1978) and Abey and Dickerson, (1983).

Kirton's (1976) Adaption-Innovation theory places individuals on a continuum of problem solving style ranging from highly adaptive to highly innovative. Adaptors seek to solve problems within established organizational guidelines while innovators seek to solve problems in new and different ways (Kirton, 1984). Kirton's adaption-innovation theory is supported by a Kirton Adaption-Innovation (KAI) inventory (Kirton, 1994). The KAI inventory has 32 questions scored with a value of one to five. The score can be further broken down into the three factors of sufficiency versus proliferation of originality (SO), reliability and efficiency (E), and rule/group conformity (R) (Kirton, 1994). The research by Scott and Bruce (1994) indicated that problem solving style has an influence on individual innovative behavior in a research and development organization.

Leader-Member exchange theory is based on the dyadic relationship between a supervisor and a subordinate (Garaen & Cashman, 1975; Graen, Novak & Scandura, 1987). High leader-member exchange members have a high degree of job latitude while low leader-member exchange members have a low degree of job latitude (Dansereauy, Graen & Haga, 1975). The quality of the relationship between a supervisor and a subordinate is related to innovativeness according to leader-member exchange theory (Graen & Scandura, 1987). The research by Scott and Bruce (1994) also indicated that the quality of the leader-member exchange has an influence on individual innovative behavior in a research and development organization.

Expectations that supervisors have for their subordinates have been suggested to shape the behavior of subordinates through the Pygmalion Effect (Livingston, 1969). Scott and Bruce (1994) theorized that managers may have expectations for subordinates that are not worked out through the leader-member exchange theory role development process. The research by Scott and Bruce (1994) indicated that a manager's expectation of individual innovative behavior for subordinates has an influence on individual innovative behavior in a research and development organization.

Several theorists believe that the work climate might channel and direct attention and action toward innovation (e.g., Amabile, 1988; Isaksen, 1987; Kanter, 1988). Several studies at both the organizational and subunit level have indicated empirical support for climate's effects on innovation (Abey & Dickerson, 1983; Paolillo & Brown, 1978; Siegel & Kaemmerer, 1978). The research by Scott and Bruce (1994) indicated that work climate has an influence on individual innovative behavior in a research and development organization.

RESEARCH QUESTION

The research question addressed in this research is, what are the determinants of individual innovative behavior in a high technology product development organization? This research follows the research performed by Scott and Bruce (1994). Scott and Bruce (1994) performed their research in a research and development organization. This research was performed in a high technology organization responsible for product development. Based on the research question and previous research on the determinants of individual innovative behavior, the six hypotheses listed below were generated. All the hypotheses in this research are from the research by Scott and Bruce (1994) except hypothesis number two. Hypothesis number two was added to investigate a relationship not previously tested but experienced by this author.

Hypothesis 1: The degree to which an individual's problem solving style is innovative is positively related to his or her innovative behavior.

Hypothesis 2: The degree to which an individual's KAI efficiency bias is positive is positively related to his or her innovative behavior.

Hypothesis 3: The quality of leader-member exchange between an individual and his or her supervisor is positively related to the individual's innovative behavior.

Hypothesis 4: The quality of leader-member exchange between an individual and his or her supervisor is positively related to the degree to which the individual perceives dimensions of climate as supportive of innovation.

Hypothesis 5: The degree to which a supervisor expects a subordinate to be innovative is positively related to subordinates' innovative behavior.

Hypothesis 6: The degree to which individuals perceive dimensions of organizational climate as supportive of innovation is positively related to their innovative behavior.

Figure 1 is a model of the proposed research indicating the relationship of the six hypotheses and innovative behavior. The factors (SO), (E), and (R) make up cognitive style or problem solving style per the KAI inventory. The factors are listed separately because this research investigates the individual component score influence on innovative behavior as well as the composite KAI inventory score. In Figure 1 the proposed relationship between innovative behavior and leader-member exchange, role expectation, climate for innovation and education is shown.

DEFINITION OF TERMS

Administrative innovations: Innovations that lead to more efficient and effective organizations. An example would be an innovative idea that led to more efficient and effective methods to track parts and materials in manufacturing process.

Causal relationship: A dependence relationship between two or more variables in which one or more variables create an outcome represented by at least one different variable in structural equation modeling (Hair, Anderson, Tathman, & Black, 1992).

Climate perception: An individual's cognitive representations of the organizational environment "expressed in terms that reflect psychologi-

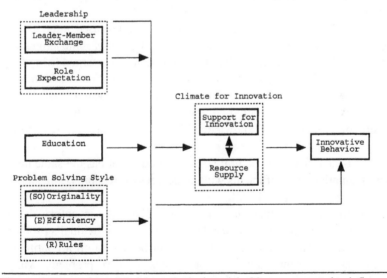

Figure 1. Research model: A hypothetical model of factors expected to influence the individual innovative behavior of individuals working in high technology product development organizations.

cally meaningful interpretations of the situation." (James, Hater, Gent, & Bruni, 1978). Climate is a cognitive interpretation of an organization, at the individual level (James, James, & Ashe, 1990).

Cronbach alpha: A measure of reliability used to evaluate a set of two or more construct indicators. The value ranges form 1.0 being best to 0.0 being worst (Hair, Anderson, Tathman, & Black, 1992).

Degrees of freedom (df): The number of bits of information available for estimating the distribution of data after all parameters have been estimated. A model with less than zero degrees of freedom can not be solved. A researcher tries to maximize the degrees of freedom while obtaining the best-fitting model (Hair, Anderson, Tathman, & Black, 1992).

Endogenous construct: A construct or variable that is the dependent or outcome variable in at least one causal relationship in structural equation modeling (Hair, Anderson, Tathman, & Black, 1992).

Exogenous construct: A construct or variable that is only a predictor for other constructs or variables in a structural equation model (Hair, Anderson, Tathman, & Black, 1992).

High technology product development organization: An organization that is responsible for the development of new high technology products for the marketplace. Four examples of high technology product development organizations are organizations that develop and manufacture jet engines, computers, avionics, and aircraft.

Innovation: Creativity and innovation are often used interchangeably in research studies (West & Farr, 1990). Recently, some agreement about the definition of creativity and innovation has emerged (Mumford & Gustafson, 1988). Innovation deals with the production or adoption of useful ideas and idea implementation (Kanter, 1988; Van de Ven, 1986). Creativity is often considered "doing something for the first time anywhere or creating new knowledge" (Woodman, Sawyer, & Griffin, 1993).

Just-identified: A structural equation model that has the same number of equations as coefficients with no degrees of freedom (Hair, Anderson, Tathman, & Black, 1992).

Kirton Adaption Innovation Inventory (KAI): An inventory, developed by M. J. Kirton in 1976, used to measure and individual's problem solving style. The results of each KAI can be placed on a continuum from adaptive to innovative. Adaptors seek to solve problems within established organizational guidelines. Innovators seek to solve problems in new and different ways (Kirton, 1976).

Latent construct or variable: These variables cannot be measured directly. In structural equation modeling these variables can be represented or measured by one or more measured variables (Hair, Anderson, Tathman, & Black, 1992). Leader Expectations: Leader/Manager expectations of subordinates' performance are passed or communicated to subordinates through the managers' behavior (Eden, 1984). Expectations that supervisors have for their subordinates have been suggested to shape the behavior of subordinates through the Pygmalion effect (Livingston, 1969).

Leader-member exchange (LMX): A theory based on the dyadic relationship between a supervisor and a subordinate (Graen & Cashman, 1975; Graen, Novak & Scandura, 1987). The relationship each subordinate develops with their supervisor will be different to create a series of dyadic relationships between the supervisor and subordinate within the work group (Graen & cashman, 1975).

Problem solving style: Is the problem solving style or cognitive style used by an individual to approach and solve problems. Problem solving style is related to several aspects or traits of personality that start early in life and are relatively stable over time. Problem solving style is assumed to be conceptually independent to cognitive capacity, success, cognitive techniques, and coping behavior (Kirton, 1989).

Process innovations: The result of process innovations are better ways to build a product. Process innovations often lead to lower production cost, more environmentally friendly production methods, and safer work environments.

Product innovations: The result of product innovations are new products for the marketplace. Product innovations are often totally new products or a better design on old products.

Reliability and efficiency (E): One of the three factors that the questions on the Kirton Adaption-Innovation Inventory load on. An individual concerned with precision, reliability, and efficiency is adaptive according to Kirton (1994). If an individual is not concerned with precision, reliability, and efficiency, they are innovative according to Kirton (1994).

Rule/group conformity (R): One of the three factors that the questions on the Kirton Adaption-Innovation Inventory load on. Adaptors like to be methodical, prudent, disciplined, and conforming while innovators like the opposite (Kirton, 1994).

Structural equation modeling (SEM): A multivariate statistical method that uses aspects of both multiple regression and factor analysis. Structural equation modeling can be used to estimate a series of interrelated dependence relationships simultaneously (Hair, Anderson, Tathman, & Black, 1992).

Sufficiency versus proliferation of originality (SO): One of the three factors that the questions on the Kirton Adaption-Innovation Inventory load on. The (SO) factor relates to an individual's preference of idea generation. Adaptors produce fewer original ideas and innovators produce more original ideas (Kirton, 1994).

Technological innovations: Innovations that lead to new technologies and make old technologies obsolete. An example is the compact disk technology.

SUMMARY

This chapter included a background discussion on innovative behavior, the purpose of this study and why this research is significant. In addition, the major streams of research and theories on innovative behavior were briefly presented and discussed. The research question, six hypotheses, and the proposed research model were also presented and briefly discussed. Finally, the definition of key terms were presented. Chapter 2 contains a more thorough discussion of the literature supporting the research question and the theoretical development of corresponding hypotheses.

Review of Literature

INTRODUCTION

In the Background section of Chapter 1, research by Kanter (1988) and Scott and Bruce (1994) on the innovation process was reviewed. Much has been written about innovation at the organizational level but "there has been scant attention paid to innovation at the individual and group levels" (West & Far, 1989). Van de Ven (1986) said that it is people in organizations who "develop, carry, react to, and modify ideas." This research is concerned with literature relating to the determinants of individual innovative behavior in high technology product development organizations.

Scott and Bruce (1994) brought together several streams of research and conducted a study on the determinants of individual innovative behavior in a research and development organization. In their research, problem solving style, leadership, and work climate were found to influence individual innovative behavior. Two of the major researchers on problem solving style reviewed in this literature review are Jabri (1991) and Kirton (1994). Leadership, in this literature review, has been broken down into leader-member exchange and innovative behavior, leader-member exchange and climate perceptions, and leader expectations and innovative behavior. Graen and Cashman (1975) and Graen, Novak and Scandura (1987) are two of the major contributors to leader-member exchange theory. Leader expectations and their influence on innovative behavior are based on an article written by Livingston (1969) and the research by Scott and Bruce (1994). Siegel and Kaemmerer (1978) are two of several researchers reviewed on the influence that work climate has on innovative behavior.

PROBLEM SOLVING STYLE AND INNOVATIVE BEHAVIOR

Researchers have recently given attention to dimensions of cognitive style that are believed to be antecedents of innovative behavior (Jabri, 1991; Kirton, 1976). Jabri (1991), developed a 19-question questionnaire that measures an individual's mode of problem solving. The 19 questions were divided into 10 in the associative dimension and 9 in the bisociative dimension. The associative dimension of thinking deals with habit or set routines that can be described in words or by symbols. The bisociative dimension of thinking deals with the combining of two or more groups of thought resulting in a nonhabitual thought. Koestler (1964), described associative thinking as single-minded mono-disciplined thinking. He described bisociative thinking as double-minded transitory thinking that involved unstable equilibrium where the balance of thought is disturbed. The research performed by Scott and Bruce (1994) supported the hypothesis that bisociative thinking is positively related to innovative behavior.

Koestler (1964), saw benefit in understanding an individual's mode of thinking at the individual and organizational levels. At the individual level one can improve his/her own problem solving abilities by understanding his/her own most recurring mode of problem solving and take positive steps toward trying other problem solving modes. A method to recognize the preferred problem solving mode is valuable at the organizational level. Koestler believed this would make it possible to select, train, and build more balanced groups. The members of the group could be selected based on individual differences in modes of problem-solving to obtain mutual benefit of the organization and group members.

A more widely accepted measure of problem solving style than the 19 question Jabri measure of problem solving style used by Scott and Bruce (1994) is the 32-question Kirton Adaption-Innovation (KAI) Inventory (Kirton, 1976). According to Scott and Bruce (1994), the Jabri (1991) problem solving style measure "is very similar in content to the more widely accepted but less accessible Kirton Adaption-Innovation measure" (KAI; Kirton, 1976). Kirton's Adaption-Innovation theory became known in 1976, when Michael Kirton wrote a paper on his Adaption-Innovation theory titled "Adaptors and Innovators: A Description and Measure" that was published in the *Journal of Applied Psychology*. He observed that people produce qualitatively different solutions to similar problems and constructed an inventory identifying adaptors from innovators. Kirton's inventory was based on personal observations, intensive interviews, and relevant literature.

It is the contention of Adaption-Innovation theory that individuals can be located on a continuum ranging from an ability to "do things better" to an ability to "do things differently." Kirton (1976) labeled the ends on the continuum adaptive and innovative respectively. One of the key assumptions of Kirton's theory is that Adaption-Innovation is a cognitive style that relates to an individual's preferred cognitive strategies related to change. Adaption-Innovation is also related to an individual's strategies of creativity, problem solving, and decision making. Another assumption of Kirton's theory is that cognitive style is related to several aspects or traits of personality that start early in life and are relatively stable over time. In Adaption-Innovation theory, cognitive style is assumed to be conceptually independent of cognitive capacity, success, cognitive techniques, and coping behavior (Kirton, 1989).

The assumption of Adaption-Innovation theory that cognitive style is distinct from cognitive capacity is gaining wider support. Kogan (1976) wrote that the level of performance is sharply different from the method of mental operation, which is dependent on how an individual acquires, stores, retrieves, and transforms information. Messick (1976) wrote that styles are based on an individual's preference for organizing and processing information, are consistent individual differences, and are congenial to the individual because style is developed around personality traits. Adaption-Innovation theory is concerned with the "how" of performance, not the performance level or success in social terms (Kirton, 1994).

Kirton believes that once cognitive style is perceived as detached from cognitive capacity it can be seen as an integral part of personality and a dimension to which groups of traits must be significantly related, as well as being interrelated. Adaption-Innovation as a cognitive style is assumed to be unrelated to level or capacity, such as IQ, level of cognitive complexity, or management competency (Kirton 1994).

Kirton (1994) believes that coping behavior is a necessary force between stable preferred cognitive styles and required behavior. A common coping behavior is based on the fact that it is possible for individuals to learn new problem-solving strategies that are not consistent with their preferred problem solving strategies but are more effective for a particular problem. Those problem solving strategies that are far removed from preferred strategies require ever-conscious effort and are abandoned as soon as possible (Kirton, 1994).

When confronted with a problem the habitual adaptor will accept the generally recognized theories, policies, customary viewpoints, and paradigms. The habitual innovator on the other hand will remove the problem from generally accepted thought and reconstruct the problem and paradigms in pursuit of solutions. Table 1 contains descriptive terms associated with adaptors and innovators taken from Kirton's (1976) article.

Adaptors seek to solve problems within established organizational guidelines. They make decisions in such a way that existing assumptions, procedures, and values of the organization are not violated. Adaptors are concerned with improving and "doing better" (Kirton, 1984). According to Drucker (1969), management is dominated by adaptors.

Innovators seek to solve problems in new and different ways. They are not concerned with the existing boundaries of the organization or definition of the problem. The implementation of an innovator's solution often challenges existing work practices and the goals and purpose of the organization. Innovators are more concerned with "doing things differently" (Kirton, 1984). For this reason innovators are often viewed by management as non-team players or trouble makers.

Table 1. Characteristics of Adaptors and Innovators

The Adaptor	The Innovator
Characterized by precision, reliability, efficiency, methodicalness, prudence, discipline, conformity.	Seen as undisciplined, thinking tangentially, approaching tasks from unsuspected angles.
Concerned with resolving residual problems thrown up by the current paradigm.	Could be said to search for problems and alternative avenues or solution, cutting across current paradigms.
Seeks solutions to problems in tried and understood ways.	Queries problems' concomitant assumptions; manipulates problems.
Reduces problems by improvement and greater efficiency, with maximum of continuity and stability.	Is catalyst to settled groups, irreverent of their consensual views; seen as abrasive, creating dissonance.

Table 1. (*cont.*)

Seen as sound, conforming, safe, dependable.	Seen as unsound, impractical; often shocks his opposite.
Liable to make goals of means.	In pursuit of goals treats accepted means with little regard.
Seems impervious to boredom, seems able to maintain high accuracy in long spells of detailed work.	Capable of detailed routine (system-maintenance) work for only short bursts.
Is an authority within given structures.	Tends to take control in unstructured situations.
Challenges rules rarely, cautiously, when assured of strong support.	Often challenges rules, has respect for past custom.
Tends to high self-doubt. Reacts to criticism by closer outward conformity. Vulnerable to social pressure and authority; compliant.	Appears to have low self-doubt when generating ideas, not needing consensus to maintain certitude in face of opposition.
Is essential to the functioning of the institution all the time, but occasionally needs to be "dug out" of his system.	In the institution is ideal in unscheduled crises, or better still to help avoid them, if he can be controlled.
When collaborating with innovators:	*When collaborating with adaptors:*
Supplies stability, order and continuity to the partnership.	Supplies the task orientations, the break with the past and accepted theory.
Is sensitive to people, maintains group cohesion and co-operation.	Appears insensitive to people, often threatens group cohesion and co-operation.
Provides a safe base for the innovator's riskier operations.	Provides the dynamics to bring about periodic radical change, without which institutions tend to ossify.

Source: Kirton, 1976.

An example of an individual with extreme innovative behavior was Charles Babbage who was born in Devonshire, England, in 1792 and died in 1871. The modern day computer is said to have started with Babbage because the mathematical principles he devised for the difference engine he created are similar to those used in advanced computers today. The difference engine is a mechanical computer that uses gears instead of electronics. Babbage was an innovative genius but never completely finished any of his mechanical computers. Babbage would come up with a better way to construct his mechanical computer before construction was ever complete on previous designs and would scrap all completed work. This trend continued at a feverish pace from 1822 to his death in 1871. After Babbage's death one of his sons completed a functional mechanical computer from his father's drawings (Morrison, P. & Morrison E., 1961).

The innovative approach is needed in organization for long term survival. Large organizations that have been successful over time must move to an adaptive orientation in an effort to prevent unacceptable risk, inherent in making drastic changes suddenly. Organizations in general have a tendency to encourage bureaucracy and adaption in an attempt to minimize risk (Kirton, 1994). Merton (1957) wrote that the goal of bureaucratic structures is precision, reliability, and efficiency. In a bureaucratic structure officials are under pressure to be methodical, prudent, and disciplined. This result is a high degree of individual conformity in bureaucracies. Individuals with these behaviors are classified as having "adaptor" personalities by Adaption-Innovation theory (Kirton, 1994).

Innovative solutions often get skeptical receptions. These solutions often have a problem with communication because the innovator often reconstructs the original problem while resolving it. The resistance to innovative ideas is reinforced by alternative solutions that are adaptive in nature and follow established paradigms. Many adaptors are seen by important others in corporations as being just as creative, resourceful, and knowledgeable as innovators and have a better reputation for being sound. Innovative proposals are often riskier than adaptive proposals because innovative proposals break down known ways and more elements are outside known experience. When innovative solutions do succeed, they are more likely to be noticed, giving glamour to the innovative thinker (Kirton, 1994).

Kirton (1976) started the development of his Adaption-Innovation theory after a study of management initiative in 1961. Kirton's objective during this study was to investigate the process by which ideas that had led to significant changes in the companies studied were developed and implemented. The significant changes in the companies studied required the cooperation of multiple managers and personnel in more than one department.

Kirton identified seven stages through which ideas go through before becoming part of the accepted routine of a company: perception of the problem; analysis of the problem; analysis of the solution; agreement to change; acceptance of change; delegation; and implementation (Kirton, 1994). During this study Kirton also examined what went wrong at the various stages and how some initiatives were blocked. Kirton found that the personalities of individuals involved at the various stages had an influence directly or indirectly on the initiative's outcome (Kirton, 1994).

Kirton discovered several anomalies during his 1961 study (Kirton, 1976). He found that the time lags in the acceptance of change varied a great deal. Some ideas took three or more years for acceptance while others were accepted with minimal analysis. Often new ideas were blocked by many management objections until a critical event or crisis occurred. Kirton observed that during a crisis situation objections and resistance to new ideas were often dropped (Kirton, 1994).

Kirton also observed that ideas generated by managers, whom themselves were not accepted by the management group, encountered heavy opposition and delays with idea implementation. This lack of an individual's acceptance often lasted even after the idea had been accepted and rated as highly successful. At the same time those managers that presented conventional ideas were themselves acceptable to the management group and remained in good standing even if their idea was rejected or failed (Kirton, 1994).

Adaption-Innovation theory offers rational and a measured explanation of Kirton's findings. Adaptive solutions are those solutions based on generally accepted paradigms. Adaptive solutions contain familiar paradigms and are more easily grasped intellectually. For this reason adaptive solutions are more readily accepted by most adaptors and those innovators not directly involved with the solution of the problem at hand. Adaptive solutions based on familiar assumptions receive limited resistance from management and are more readily acceptable (Kirton, 1994).

When an idea submitted by an adaptor fails, the blame can often be written off as "bad luck" or due to "unforeseeable events" because the idea was based on shared assumptions and paradigms. The innovator, on the other hand, is likely to base solutions on ideas not as closely related to generally accepted assumptions and paradigms. For this reason innovative ideas are often met with resistance and the innovator is liable to be treated with suspicion and derision (Schoen, 1960).

Hayward and Evertt (1983) made a study using the KAI in a local authority setting. The local authority studied had recently set up a new section under unusual lines for such an authority by utilizing an entrepreneur as the section manager. Adaption-Innovation theory predicts that the mean value of the Kirton Adaption-Innovation inventory for local government managers would be toward the adaptive pole. The mean of senior management was found to be 79.5 and the mean of all levels was found to be 86.0. Both of the mean scores are well below the general population mean of 95 as predicted by Adaption-Innovation theory (Hayward & Everett, 1983).

Hayward and Everett (1983) found that the establishment of the innovative profit-making section within the highly adaptive authority caused much suspicion and resistance from established management. It was observed that when the entrepreneur section became patently more successful, resistance to this section increased. Tolerance for the entrepreneur section from the adaptive establishment was reduced with their success. Hayward and Everett (1983) presumed that the success of the entrepreneur section put pressure on the adaptive establishment and lower tolerance for the entrepreneur section was their response.

The instrument used to measure the level of Adaption-Innovation, the KAI inventory, is not a measure of cognitive or intellectual level. The KAI should not be confused with concepts such as level of creativity, capacity for cognitive complexity or extent of some ability. Adaption-Innovation theory is useful for understanding behavior in a variety of situations. This theory concerns the manner or the method of performance, not the level of effectiveness of performance or its success in social terms. An understanding of Adaptor-Innovator theory can provide useful insight to individuals in understanding how they work and why others may have styles that are different from theirs (Kirton, 1994).

The Kirton Adaption-Innovation Inventory (KAI) is the instrument on which much of the demonstration of Adaption-Innovation theory relies (Kirton, 1976). This instrument produces a score that places adaptors and innovators on a continuum. The KAI inventory is a one page instrument that has 33 items. One of the 33 items is a control item and is not scored, leaving 32 items (Kirton, 1987).

The respondents taking the inventory are instructed "to imagine that they had been asked to present, consistently and for a long time, a certain image of themselves to others" (Kirton, 1976). Respondents are instructed to "state the degree of difficulty that such a task would entail for them" for each of the 33 items on a five point scale ranging from very hard to very easy (Kirton, 1976). Table 2 lists the 32 scored items in the KAI inventory. The response to each of the KAI inventory items is scored with a whole number ranging from 1 to 5. This gives a theoretical minimum score of 32 and a maximum score of 160. The observed range of the KAI based on more than 1,000 subjects is a low of 45 and a high of 146. Kirton (1976) arbitrarily defined the 32 end of the continuum as adaptive and the 160 end of the continuum as innovative. Several of the items in the KAI inventory are reverse scored to avoid response set (Kirton, 1987).

The theoretical mean for KAI inventory responses is a score of 96. The mean for the general population was found to be 95 with a normal curve distribution. Other general population samples in the USA and Italy resulted in similar KAI Scores (Kirton, 1994). Hayward and Everett (1983) administered the KAI inventory in a bureaucratic local authority setting and found the KAI mean of upper management to be an adaptive 79.5, as KAI theory would predict.

A study by Kirton and Pender (1982) investigated the KAI inventory results from 2,375 subjects collected in 15 independent studies. In this study Engineers had an adaptive mean KAI score of 86.5 while research and development personnel had an innovative mean KAI score of 101.8. These findings support the theory that "mean scores on the Kirton Adaption-Innovation Inventory are more innovative for occupational groups which deal with more numerous and less rigid paradigms" (Kirton, M.J. & Pender, S., 1982).

Innovation deals with the production or adoption of useful ideas and idea implementation (Kanter, 1988; Vande Ven, 1986). The innovative problem solving style individual is less bound to existing paradigms and is more self directed to the development of novel problem solutions than the adaptive problem solving style individual. The research by Scott and Bruce (1994) supported the hypothesis that "the degree which an individual's problem-solving style is intuitive is positively related to his or her innovative behavior." A similar hypothesis using the more widely accepted Kirton Adaption-Innovation theory is Hypothesis 1.

Hypothesis 1: The degree to which an individual's problem solving style is innovative is positively related to his or her innovative behavior.

Table 2. Items in the Kirton Adaption-Innovation Inventory, or KAI

1.	Has original ideas
2.	Proliferates ideas
3.	Is stimulating
4.	Copes with several new ideas at the same time
5.	Will always think of something when stuck
6.	Would sooner create than improve
7.	Has fresh perspectives on old problems
8.	Often risks doing things differently
9.	Likes to vary set routines at a moment's notice
10.	Prefers to work on one problem at a time
11.	Can stand out in disagreement against group
12.	Needs the stimulation of frequent change
13.	Prefers changes to occur gradually
14.	Is thorough
15.	Masters all details painstakingly
16.	Is methodical and systematic
17.	Enjoys detailed work
18.	Is (not) a steady plodder
19.	Is consistent
20.	Imposes strict order on matters within own control
21.	Fits readily into "the system"
22.	Conforms
23.	Readily agrees with the team at work
24.	Never seeks to bend or break the rules
25.	Never acts without proper authority
26.	Is prudent when dealing with authority
27.	Likes the protection of precise instructions
28.	Is predictable
29.	Prefers colleagues who never "rock the boat"
30.	Likes bosses and work patterns which are consistent
31.	Works without deviation in a prescribed way
32.	Holds back ideas until obviously needed

Source: Kirton, 1976.

The 32 items in the KAI inventory can be further broken down into the three sub groups or factors, sufficiency versus proliferation of originality (SO), reliability and efficiency (E), and rule/group conformity (R)(Kirton, 1994). The first 13 of the KAI inventory items listed in Table 2 loaded on the (SO) factor. The next 7 items loaded on the (E) factor and the remaining 12 items loaded on the (R) factor (Kirton, 1976). Each of the 32 items on the KAI are scored on a scale from one to five. Kirton found that participants taking the KAI generally scored consistently adaptive or innovative in each of the three subgroups (Kirton, 1994). The expected KAI score for the (SO) subgroup would be 13/32 times the total KAI score, the (E) subgroup would be 7/32 times the total KAI score, and the (R) subgroup would be 12/32 times the total KAI score.

The (SO) factor has been labeled Sufficiency versus Proliferation of originality by Kirton (1994). The (SO) factor has similarities to Rogers' (1959) work of the "creative loner." According to Kirton (1994) adaptors prefer the generation of fewer original ideas that are sound, useful and relevant to the problem as they see it. Innovators on the other hand proliferate ideas and compulsively toy with ideas. At the extremes of the adaption-innovation continuum adaptors produce too few original ideas to insure that some will be radical and paradigm-cracking while innovators produce so many ideas that it is hard to choose a good and acceptable solution (Kirton, 1994). The (SO) originality factor relates to an individual's preference of idea generation and should not be confused with level or capacity required to produce solutions (Kirton, 1994).

The second factor (E) is in line with Weber's (1970) study of the goals of bureaucratic structure (Kirton, (1987). Webber concentrated primarily on the adaptor side of the adaption-innovation continuum. Weber characterized bureaucrats as being concerned with precision, reliability, and efficiency. According to Kirton (1994) innovation is rarely efficient at first and can be a discontinuous process. An individual concerned with precision, reliability, and efficiency is adaptive according to Kirton (1994). If an individual is not concerned with precision, reliability, and efficiency, they are innovative according to Kirton (1994).

The third factor (R) has been labeled rule/group conformity (Kirton, 1994). This factor has similarities to the analysis by Merton (1957) of bureaucratic structure. Merton's analysis indicated that the bureaucratic structure pressured individuals to be methodical, prudent, and disciplined, and to a high degree of conformity. The qualities described by Merton lead to high adaptive behavior (Kirton, 1994). Innovators prefer to resist such bureaucratic pressures and pursue the development of their own ideas (Kirton, 1994).

Recently this researcher scored a KAI inventory from an individual that is innovative per the definition of innovative behavior given in Chapter 1. This definition is that innovation and innovative behavior deals with the production or adoption of useful ideas and idea implementation (Kanter, 1988: Van de Ven, 1986). The KAI inventory scores for this individual were 59 (SO), 16 (E), and 51 (R) for a total KAI score or 126. The equivalent or normalized KAI score for (SO), (R), and (E) is 145, 73, and 136 respectively. With 95 being the average KAI score the (E) score is on the extreme adaptive side of the KAI continuum while the (SO) and (R) scores are on the extreme innovative side of the KAI continuum. The results of this KAI inventory were brought to the attention of M.J. Kirton (personal communication, February 28, 1996) during a KAI certification class. Kirton said it is uncommon for the normalized KAI scores of the three factor groups to vary a great deal from each other on the adaption-innovation continuum.

This research investigates the research KAI inventory results to better understand if this KAI score is an anomaly or if there is some relationship with individual innovative behavior. An individual with adaptive (E) and innovative (SO) and (E) could be beneficial for innovative behavior. An individual with adaptive (E) would be concerned with precision, reliability and efficiency. Due to extreme complexity, many recent innovations in high technology industries would not come to fruition without precision, reliability and efficiency. Complicated technologies based on years of data and experience require precision, reliability, and efficiency from innovative individuals to generate innovative ideas. Without precision, reliability, and efficiency, innovative individuals may never complete innovative solutions before the competition does.

Individuals with innovative (SO) proliferate ideas and compulsively toy with ideas (Kirton, 1994). This individual would evaluate every angle of a problem to generate innovative solutions. An individual with innovative (R) would not conform to existing paradigms or established rules and would have a better chance than an adaptive (R) to generate new innovative solution that break existing paradigms. Hypothesis 2 was generated to test the relationship between the magnitude that an individual's normalized (E) score on the adaption-innovation continuum is lower than his/her averaged, normalized (SO) and (R) score on the adaption-innovation continuum and innovative behavior. The KAI (SO), (E), and (R) scores were normalized by factoring by 32/13, 32/7, and 32/12 respectively. The value of an individual's averaged, normalized (SO) and (R) score minus normalized (E) score was termed KAI efficiency bias.

Hypothesis 2: The degree to which an individual's KAI efficiency bias is positive is positively related to his or her innovative behavior.

LEADERSHIP AND INNOVATIVE BEHAVIOR

Many articles have indicated a direct connection between leadership and the innovation process (Scott & Bruce, 1994). Some of these articles have focused on the need for participative or collaborative leadership styles (Kanter, 1983; Pelz & Andrews, 1966). Other articles have concentrated on lists of activities that leaders should do in order for innovation to emerge (Amabile, 1988). Theoretical development of the relationship between leadership and innovation is weak when compared to the theoretical development between leadership and productivity (Waldman & Bass, 1991).

Scott and Bruce (1994) investigated the relationship between two contemporary leadership approaches and individual innovative behavior. The Leader-Member Exchange (LMX) theory (Dansereau, Graen, & Haga, 1975; Graen & Scandura, 1987) was used by Scott and Bruce because it had previously been connected to innovation (Scott & Bruce, 1994). The second leadership approach investigated was the effect of role expectations on innovative behavior due to the "Pygmalion effect" (Livingston, 1969). Scott and Bruce were the first to test this relationship between the Pygmalion effect and innovative behavior (Scott & Bruce, 1994). The Pygmalion effect is the change in one individual's behavior due to the expectations for that behavior he/she received from another (Eden, 1984).

Leader-Member Exchange and Innovative Behavior

Leader-Member Exchange theory is based on the dyadic relationship between a supervisor and a subordinate (Graen & Cashman, 1975; Graen, Novak, & Scandura, 1987). Over time it is theorized that supervisors develop relationships with each of their subordinates through role-making. Each relationship developed will be different to create a series of dyadic relationships between the supervisor and subordinate within the work group (Graen & Cashman, 1975). Research has indicated that high leader-member exchange members have a high degree of job latitude, while low leader-member exchange members have a low degree of job latitude (Dansereau, Graen & Haga, 1975). High leader-member exchange members have more autonomy, flexibility to do their work, and leader-delegated decision-making authority (Garen & Cashman, 1975).

Consistent patterns have emerged from the research on the leader-member dyads in leader-member exchange theory. A member will commit himself/herself to a higher level of performance and responsibility than required by job description. In exchange, the member receives positional resources such as privileged information or challenging projects (Graen, Novak & Sommerkamp, 1982).

Dyadic leadership is strongest during the mature stage of leader-member exchange. At the mature stage, the valued roles have been routinized and the dyad members reach an understanding of their role for the relationship (Graen & Scandura, 1987). Not all supervisor-subordinate relationships will advance to the mature stage (Dansereau, Graen, & Haga, 1975). Problems such as organizational constraints, or inability to find valued exchange agents can limit leader-member exchange quality (Graen & Scandura, 1987). A study by Graen, Novak, and Sommerkamp (1982) indicates that the quality of the leader-member exchange can be improved significantly through training.

The quality of the relationship between a supervisor and a subordinate is related to innovativeness according to leader-member exchange theory (Graen & Scandura, 1987). It is believed that supervisors and subordinates take part in a role development process during which the amount of decision latitude, influence, and autonomy the subordinate is allowed are established (Graen & Cashman, 1975). Supervisor and subordinate relationships that are characterized by trust, mutual liking, respect, autonomy, and decision latitude have been shown to be critical to innovative behavior (Cotgrove & Box, 1970; Pelz & Andrews, 1966). Limited research performed on the relationship between leader-member exchange and innovation has supported a positive relationship (Scott & Bruce, 1994). Scott and Bruce (1994) introduced Hypothesis 1, for the relationship between leader-member exchange and individual innovative behavior. The research performed by Scott and Bruce (1994) in a research and development organization indicated significant support for Hypothesis 3.

Hypothesis 3: The quality of leader-member exchange between an individual and his or her supervisor is positively related to the individual's innovative behavior.

Leader-Member Exchange and Climate Perception

Scott and Bruce (1994) hypothesized that leader-member exchange influenced innovative behavior indirectly through an influence on the formation of climate perceptions. Kozlowski and Doherty (1989) integrated the research on leader-member exchange theory and the existing research on climate. They argued that because supervisors are the most direct and visible representatives of management actions, policies, and procedures, subordinates often generalize their perceptions of supervisors to the organization as a whole (Kozlowski & Doherty, 1989). Thus, "subordinates successfully negotiating high quality relationships with their supervisors will perceive their organization as providing greater autonomy, decision-making latitude, and supportiveness overall than will subordinates with low-quality relationships with their supervisors" (Scott & Bruce, 1994).

A positive relationship between leader-member exchange quality and climate perceptions has been empirically supported (Dunegan, Tierney, Duchon, 1992; Kozlowski & Doherty, 1989). Scott and Bruce (1994) introduced hypothesis 4, for the relationship between leader-member exchange and climate for innovation. The research performed by Scott and Bruce (1994) in a research and development organization indicated significant support for Hypothesis 4.

> Hypothesis 4: The quality of leader-member exchange between an individual and his or her supervisor is positively related to the degree to which the individual perceives dimensions of climate as supportive of innovation.

Leader Expectations and Innovative Behavior

Scott and Bruce (1994) theorized that managers may have expectations for subordinates that are not worked out through the leader-member exchange theory role development process. Some managers may have rigid expectations for specific roles within their control or may lack interest in or enough imagination to guide subordinates' role with a task (Graen & Scandura, 1987). Expectations that supervisors have for their subordinates have been suggested to shape the behavior of subordinates through the Pygmalion effect (Livingston, 1969). An article by Eden (1984) theorized that manager's expectations of subordinates' performance are passed or communicated to subordinates through the managers' behaviors. Scott and Bruce (1994) theorized that when managers expect subordinates to be innovative, subordinates will perceive the managers as encouraging and facilitating their innovative effort. These behaviors will be seen as representative of their organizations at large, and therefore the organizations will be perceived as supportive of innovation.

Scott and Bruce (1994) introduced Hypothesis 5 for the relationship between supervisor expectations and innovative behavior. The research performed by Scott and Bruce (1994) in a research and development organization indicated significant support for Hypothesis 5.

Hypothesis 5: The degree to which a supervisor expects a subordinate to be innovative is positively related to subordinate's innovative behavior.

WORK CLIMATE AND INNOVATIVE BEHAVIOR

One of the biggest problems in managing innovation is the management of attention (Van de Ven, 1986). This is difficult because individuals adapt to their environments over time in such a way that their awareness of the need for change is minimized. They get to a point where only a crisis situation will stimulate action (Scott & Bruce, 1994). Several theorists believe that the work climate might channel and direct attention and action toward innovation (e.g., Amabile, 1988; Isaksen, 1987; Kanter, 1988). James, Hater, Gent, and Bruni (1978) defined climate as an individual's cognitive representations of the organizational environment "expressed in terms that reflect psychologically meaningful interpretations of the situation." Scott and Bruce (1994) posited that "leadership, work group relations and problem solving style affect individual innovative behavior directly and indirectly through perceptions of a climate for innovation." Climate has an effect on innovation at organizational, subunit, and individual levels within an organization (Scott & Bruce, 1994). Several studies at both the organizational and subunit level have indicated empirical support for climate's effects on innovation (Abey & Dickson, 1983; Paolillo & Brown, 1978; Siegel & Kaemmerer, 1978). Empirical studies of climates' effects on individual innovative behavior have been carried out by a limited number of researchers (Amabile & Gryskiewicz, 1989; Scott & Bruce, 1994).

Climate is a cognitive interpretation of an organization, at the individual level, that has been labeled "psychological climate" (James, James, & Ashe, 1990). In psychological climate theory, individuals respond primarily to cognitive representations of environments "rather than to the environments per se" (James & Sells, 1981). Climate represents the signals employees receive from organizations concerning expectations for behavior and potential outcomes of behavior (Scott & Bruce, 1994). Individuals use information from climate to formulate expectancies and instrumentalities (James, Hartman, Stebbins, & Jones, 1977). It is also believed that employees respond to these expectations by controlling their behavior such that positive self-evaluative consequences, such as self-satisfaction and self-pride, are realized (Bandura, 1988).

There are many types of climates and "to speak of organizational climate per se, without attaching a referent, is meaningless" (Schneider & Reichers, 1983). A study of innovative performance among R&D units, by Abbey and Dickson, only two of the work-climate dimensions studied, performance-reward dependency and flexibility, were consistently correlated with R&D innovation (Abbey & Dickson, 1983). Abbey and Dickson concluded that rewards given in recognition of excellent performance and organizational willingness to experiment with innovative ideas were characteristics of innovative R&D unit climates.

Other researchers have noted additional climate factors that are characteristic of innovative organizations. Organizational orientation toward creativity and innovative change and support for those working independently in the pursuit of new ideas were found to be critical (Kanter, 1983; Siegel & Kaemmerer, 1978). A tolerance for diversity among members of the organization was found to be important (Siegel & Kaemmerer, 1978). Adequate supplies of critical resources such as equipment, facilities and time were found to be critical to innovation (Amabile, 1988; Angle, 1989; Taylor, 1963).

Empirical research has supported the effect that climate has on organizational and departmental innovation. Scott and Bruce (1994) introduced Hypothesis 6, for the relationship between organizational climate and individual innovative behavior. The research performed by Scott and Bruce (1994) in a research and development organization indicated significant support for Hypothesis 6.

Hypothesis 6: The degree to which individuals perceive dimensions of organizational climate as supportive of innovation is positively related to their innovative behavior.

SUMMARY

There has been a large amount of research on the antecedents of creativity, innovation, and organizational climate. Scott and Bruce (1994) integrated a number of independent research streams and then developed and tested a theoretical model of individual innovative behavior in a research and development organization. This research found problem solving style, leader-member exchange, leader expectations and work climate to be positively related to individual innovative behavior (Scott & Bruce, 1994). This research extends the Scott and Bruce (1994) research beyond the research and development organization.

Kirton Adaption-Innovation theory places individuals on a continuum of problem solving style from adaptive to innovative (Kirton, 1976). Adaptive individuals seek to solve problems within established organizational guidelines and paradigms. Adaptors make decisions in such a way that existing assumptions, procedures, and values of the organization are not violated. Innovative individuals on the other hand seek to solve problems in new and different ways. The implementation of an innovator's solution often challenges existing work practices and the goals and purpose of the organization (Kirton, 1994). Break through paradigm cracking innovation is more likely with a highly innovative individual according to Kirton Adaption-Innovation theory (Kirton, 1994).

Kirton (1994) wrote that problem solving style is established early in life and is stable over time. Problem solving style is independent of capacity or IQ. Koestler (1964) believed that knowledge of an individual's problem solving style is valuable because this would make it possible to select, train, and build more balanced groups. Knowledge and understanding of the influence that problem solving style has on individual innovative behavior would give managers a tool to more effectively staff project teams.

Leader-member exchange theory by Graen and Cashman (1975) and Graen and Scandura (1987) was used by Scott and Bruce (1994). In this research a positive relationship was established between the quality of the leader-member exchange and individual innovative behavior in a research and development organization. In leader-member exchange theory it is theorized that supervisors develop relationships with each of their subordinates through role-making. High leader-member exchange members have a high degree of job latitude while low leader-member exchange members have a low degree of job latitude (Dansereau, Graen & Haga, 1975). It is theorized that high quality leader-member exchange members are more innovative because they are allowed more autonomy, flexibility to do their work, and leader-delegated decision-making authority (Garen & Cashman, 1975).

Scott and Bruce (1994) theorized that leader-member exchange influenced innovative behavior indirectly through an influence on the formation of climate perceptions. Positive relationships between leader-member exchange and climate perceptions have been empirically supported (Dunegan, Tierney, Duchon; Kozlowski & Doherty, 1989; Scott & Bruce, 1994). Management can influence the quality of the leader-member exchange in an organization by strategically choosing supervisors and through training (Novak & Sommerkamp, 1982).

The expectations that supervisors have for their subordinates have been suggested to shape the behavior of subordinates through the Pygmalion effect (Livingston, 1969). The research by Scott and Bruce (1994) indicated a positive relationship between supervisor expectations and innovative behavior. The Scott and Bruce (1994) study indicates that managers can increase the innovative behavior of subordinates by increasing innovative expectations of subordinates.

Several theorist believe that the work climate can channel and direct attention and action toward innovation (e.g., Amabile, 1988; Isaksen, 1987; Kanter, 1988). Organizational orientation toward creativity and innovative change and support for those working independently in the pursuit of new ideas were found to be critical for innovative behavior (Kanter, 1983; Siegel & Kaemmerer, 1978). The research by Scott and Bruce (1994) indicated a positive relationship between the degree to which individuals perceive dimensions of organizational climate as supportive of innovation and innovative behavior. The Scott and Bruce (1994) research study indicates that managers can increase innovative behavior by improving the work climate for innovative behavior.

The research by Scott and Bruce (1994) indicates that management can have a positive impact on individual innovative behavior within an organization. By selecting individuals with the best problem solving style for a project, improving leader-member exchange, increasing leader expectation and improving the work climate for innovation, managers can have a positive influence on individual innovative behavior. This research extends the Scott and Bruce (1994) research from a research and development organization to a high technology product development organization. In Chapter 3, the methodology used to test the six hypotheses given in this chapter in a high technology product development organization is reviewed.

Methodology

OVERVIEW

In this chapter the methodology used to evaluate the determinants of individual innovative behavior in a high technology product development organization is reviewed. A review and brief summary of the research question presented in Chapter 1 is given. The six null hypotheses and the six research hypotheses used to investigate the research question are listed. The statistical methods used to test and evaluate the six null hypotheses are reviewed. The measures used in this research to evaluate research parameters are described and reviewed. An overview of the company used in this research and the procedures used to administer this research are reviewed.

RESEARCH QUESTION AND SUPPORTING HYPOTHESES

The research question addressed in this research is: What are the determinants of individual innovative behavior in a high technology product development organization? Included in Chapter 2, "Review of Literature," is a review of research and literature on the determinants of individual innovative behavior. In a research study by Scott and Bruce (1994), in a research and development organization, problem solving style, leadership, climate for innovation, and role expectation were found to be positively related to individual innovative behavior. The question investigated by this research is, do the same positive relationships between individual innovative behavior and problem solving style, leadership, climate for innovation, and role expectations hold for high technology product development organizations? The research question is tested with the six null hypotheses listed next.

Null Hypothesis 1: The degree to which an individual's problem solving style is innovative is either negatively related or not related to his or her innovative behavior.

Null Hypothesis 2: The degree to which an individual's KAI efficiency bias is positive is either negatively related or not related to his or her innovative behavior.

Null Hypothesis 3: The quality of leader-member exchange between an individual and his or her supervisor is either negatively related or not related to the individual's innovative behavior.

Null Hypothesis 4: The quality of leader-member exchange between an individual and his or her supervisor is either negatively related or not related to the degree to which the individual perceives dimensions of climate as supportive of innovation.

Null Hypothesis 5: The degree to which a supervisor expects a subordinate to be innovative is either negatively related or not related to subordinates' innovative behavior.

Null Hypothesis 6: The degree to which individuals perceive dimensions of organizational climate as supportive of innovation is either negatively related or not related to their innovative behavior.

All but one of the research hypotheses were taken from the research by Scott and Bruce (1994). Research Hypothesis 2 was added to investigate a relationship not previously tested but experienced by this researcher. The six research hypotheses are listed next.

Hypothesis 1: The degree to which an individual's problem solving style is innovative is positively related to his or her innovative behavior.

Hypothesis 2: The degree to which an individual's KAI efficiency bias is positive is positively related to his or her innovative behavior.

Hypothesis 3: The quality of leader-member exchange between an individual and his or her supervisor is positively related to the individual's innovative behavior.

Hypothesis 4: The quality of leader-member exchange between an individual and his or her supervisor is positively related to the degree to which the individual perceives dimensions of climate as supportive of innovation.

Hypothesis 5: The degree to which a supervisor expects a subordinate to be innovative is positively related to subordinates' innovative behavior.

Hypothesis 6: The degree to which individuals perceive dimensions of organizational climate as supportive of innovation is positively related to their innovative behavior.

MEASURES

Several measures were used in this research. Included in Table 3 is a summary of study measures, listing of the source of data and the measures used. This table lists the number of questions included in each measure. The measures are also broken down into independent, demographic and dependent variables.

Problem Solving Style

Problem solving style was measured using the Kirton Adaption-Innovation inventory form. Officially copyrighted KAI response sheets were used in this research. The KAI response sheet is a one page form with eight write in demographic blanks and 33 KAI inventory questions. One of the 33 questions is not scored leaving 32 scored questions.

Respondents are asked to "imagine that they had been asked to present, consistently and for a long time, a certain image of themselves to others" (Kirton, 1976). They were then asked to rate the degree of difficulty they would have with each of the 33 items on a five-point scale ranging from very easy to very hard (Kirton, 1976). A person who has original ideas, a person who enjoys detailed work, and a person who conforms, are a sampling of the 33 questions included in the KAI Inventory (Kirton, 1976).

The theoretical score on the KAI ranges from 32 to 160. Kirton (1976) arbitrarily choose the high score on the KAI inventory to represent the Innovative pole of the Adaption-Innovation continuum and the low score to represent the adaptive pole. Several of the questions are reverse coded so a response with too many "very easy responses" is sus-

Table 3. Summary of Study Measures

MEASURE	SOURCE OF DATA
INDEPENDENT VARIABLES:	
PROBLEM SOLVING STYLE Kirton, Adaption-Innovation Inventory, Kirton (1987)	32 questions administered to all Subordinates
LEADERSHIP Leader-Member Exchange Graen, et al,. (1982) Graen & Scandura (1987)	14 questions administered to all Subordinates
CLIMATE FOR INNOVATION Siegel and Kaemmerer (1978) Scott and Bruce (1994)	22 questions administered to all Subordinates
ROLE EXPECTATION Scott and Bruce (1994)	1 question evaluated by Manager/Supervisor of Each Subordinate
DEMOGRAPHIC VARIABLES:	
Kirton, Adaption-Innovation Inventory, Kirton (1987)	8 items filled in by all Subordinates
DEPENDENT VARIABLES:	
INNOVATIVE BEHAVIOR Scott and Bruce (1994)	6 questions evaluated by Manager/Supervisor of each Subordinate

Source: Adapted from Scott & Bruce (1994) and Tierney (1992).

pect. Test scores from about 1,000 subjects had a KAI test score range of 45 to 146 with a mean score of 95 (Kirton, 1994). The Cronbach alpha for a sample of 562 was 0.88 (Kirton, 1976).

Leadership

The quality of the relationship between Engineers, Designers, and Technicians and manager/supervisor was measured using the 14 item measure developed by Graen, Novak, and Sommerkanp (1982). The Leader-Member Exchange questionnaire used in this research is an adaptation by Tierney (1992) of the work by Graen, et al. (1982) and Graen and Scandura (1987).

The 14 items on the Leader-Member Exchange questionnaire were scored using a five-point scale. Some of the questions included in this measure are: (1) How well did your supervisor understand your job problems and needs? (2) How well did your supervisor recognize your potential? (3) How often did you share your good ideas with your supervisor? In research by Tierney (1992) the Cronbach alpha for the proposed questionnaire was 0.91. The Cronbach alpha for the research sample of 74 Engineers, Designers, and Technicians in this research was 0.93.

Climate for Innovation

The climate for innovation measure used in this research is an adaptation by Scott and Bruce (1994) of work by Siegel and Kaemmerer (1978) and Pritchand and Karasick (1973). This measure contains 22 questions. The survey questions measuring "resource supply" are the six questions 14 through 19. Eleven of the 22 questions were reverse coded. All responses values were entered into the research data base with favorable work environment being higher than unfavorable. Respondents were asked to answer each question as it applies to their present work environment. The scale used was a five-point scale ranging from strongly disagree to strongly agree. Some of the questions included in this measure are: (1) Creativity is encouraged here; (2) around here a person can get in a lot of trouble by being different; (3) assistance in developing new ideas is readily available; (4) this organization publicly recognizes those who are innovative.

Scott and Bruce (1994) determined that the 22 questions in their climate for innovation measure loaded on two factors. The first factor was named "support for innovation" and the second factor was named "resource supply" with 16 and 6 items respectively (Scott & Bruce, 1994). In their research the Cronbach alpha for the first factor was 0.92 and for the second factor 0.77. The Cronbach alpha in this research sample of 74 Engineers, Designers, and Technicians was 0.88 and 0.63 for "support for innovation" and "resource supply" respectively. The Cronbach alpha for the combined 22 questions for the research sample of 74 Engineers, Designers, and Technicians was 0.87.

Role Expectation

The role expectation that the manager/supervisor has for each Engineer, Designer, or Technician was measured using the following question developed by Scott and Bruce (1994).

> Not all work roles require individuals to be innovative. In fact, it could be argued that effective work groups have a blend of innovative individuals and individuals whose *role* it is to support the innovation of others. In this context, the role is a set of expectations of the position independent of the person holding the position. Indicate the degree to which you would describe the role for each of your subordinates as being either an innovator or being a supporter of innovation.

The manager/supervisor of each subordinate was asked to rate each engineer on a five-point scale ranging from "role requires an innovator" to "role requires a supporter." The question was reverse coded with "role requires an innovator" scored with a value of one on the questionnaire. The score was reversed before it was entered into the research data base to make "role requires an innovator" a value of five. This is in line with the KAI scoring where arbitrarily the innovative individual has a higher score than the adaptive individual. Scott and Bruce (1994) tested this measure 14 months after the first testing and test-retest reliability was 0.87.

Demographic Data

The demographic data was taken directly from the KAI inventory response sheet. Respondents were asked to fill in the eight demographic items before starting on the 33 KAI inventory questions. The eight items were Date, Name, Age, Sex, Occupation/Title, Department, Educational Status, and Other. The respondents age in years was not changed before data analysis. The Engineering departments were broken down into six departments. The following values were assigned to the six departments: Lab Technicians, 1; Designers, 2; Application Engineers, 3; Technical Support Engineers, 4; Product Engineers, 5; and Engineering Management, 6. Education levels were assigned the following values: high school, 1; some college, 2; associate degree, 3; bachelor's degree, 4; master's degree, 5; and Ph.D. degree, 6.

Innovative Behavior

The degree of innovative behavior exhibited by each subordinate was measured by their manager's/supervisor's response to six items. The six items were developed and used by Scott and Bruce (1994) in their research on the determinants of innovative behavior in a research and development organization. Scott and Bruce (1994) based the six items on the work by Kanter (1988) and personal interviews with company managers. The innovative behavior questionnaire by Scott and Bruce (1994) starts out with the following information about innovative behavior.

> Innovation is a process involving both the generation and implementation of ideas. As such, it requires a wide variety of specific behaviors on the part of individuals. While some people might be expected to exhibit all the behaviors involved in innovation, others may exhibit only one or a few types of behavior. Please rate each of your subordinates on the extent to which he or she:

Managers/Supervisors rated each of their subordinates on a five-point Likert-type scale ranging from "not at all" to "to an exceptional degree."

The six questions used in this research are listed next (Scott & Bruce, 1994).

1. Searches out new technologies, processes techniques, and/or product ideas
2. Generates creative ideas
3. Promotes and champions ideas to others
4. Investigates and secures funds needed to implement new ideas
5. Develops adequate plans and schedules for the implementation of new ideas
6. Is innovative

Scott and Bruce (1994) found the Cronbach alpha for their Innovative Behavior questionnaire to be 0.89. The Cronbach alpha for the research sample of 74 Engineers, Designers, and Technicians was 0.94.

Scott and Bruce (1994) tested the relationship between their Innovative Behavior questionnaire and company records of invention disclosures filed. They totaled up the number of invention disclosures filed for each individual and divided this number by the number of years of employment. This objective value was correlated with the results of their

Innovative Behavior questionnaire. Scott and Bruce (1994) found the correlation to be significant at 0.33 (p < 0.001).

SAMPLE AND SETTING

The company surveyed in this research will be referred to as XYZ Company to keep the source of information confidential. This company is responsible for the engineering, design, production, service, and sales of high technology products in a global marketplace. Competition is intense in the world marketplace, and only the strong survive. About two years ago XYZ Company received a new president who has since been pushing the company to be more innovative. He believes the way to survival in the competitive high technology world market is through more innovative people. As part of a plan to be more innovative, all the top management in Engineering has changed in the past two years. Allowing this researcher to study innovative behavior in their organization is another indication that this company truly wants to be more innovative.

Another push to be more innovative has been to bring new technology into the Design Department and the Testing Lab. The Design Department was in the process of switching from two-dimensional to three-dimensional computer drawings at the time of this research. There are many advantages to three-dimensional drafting but designers must first learn new computer software and drafting even simple parts can be difficult. The Testing Lab was in the final process of switching from human to computer data collection. This put pressure on the Testing Lab personnel for two reasons. First, Lab Technicians must become proficient with computers and electronic testing equipment to be effective on the job. Second, fewer Lab Technicians are required because twenty-four hour testing can now be performed by a computer in off-hours.

This research was conducted in the Engineering Department of Company XYZ. All Engineers, Designers, and Technicians were asked to take part in this innovation research. The Engineering Department has 61 Engineers, 17 Designers, and 28 Technicians for a total of 106 individuals.

PROCEDURE

This researcher worked with the Director of Technology to administer research questionnaires. The Director of Technology sent e-mail messages to all Engineers, Designers, and Technicians informing them that it was mandatory that they attend a scheduled innovation research meeting.

At the innovation research meeting this researcher distributed a subordinate research package consisting of the KAI inventory, the Leader-Member Exchange survey, and the Climate for Innovation survey to all present. Managers/Supervisors were given a one page Innovative Behavior and Role Expectation survey to be filled out for each of their subordinates.

At the research meeting this researcher was introduced as the researcher who was going to carry out innovation research at XYZ Company. This researcher thanked everyone in advance for taking part in this management research concerning innovation. Respondents were asked to be honest and open with all survey responses. The only wrong answer is one that does not best describe them or their situation. Confidentiality of all survey responses was promised. Participants were assured that no individual survey results would be shared with Company XYZ management, only general statistical information would be presented. The importance of the demographic data in the upper left hand corner of the KAI inventory, especially their name, was stressed. This researcher informed them that their name was needed to pair their survey response with a short survey response by their manager/supervisor. Their name would also be used to send them their KAI Adaption-Innovation inventory results in a sealed envelope with a KAI feedback summary form. Respondents were further assured that their names would be removed from the research data base once their response was paired with their supervisor's response. All respondents were again thanked for their participation and honesty on survey responses before the research surveys were administered.

Subordinate survey responses were collected before they left the meeting room. A total of 88 subordinate survey packages were received at the research meeting. Only one of the 88 respondents failed to put their name on the survey response. The Director of Research agreed to collect more subordinate survey responses from those not present and to collect manager/supervisor responses. A total of four subordinate survey packages were received by mail in confidential envelopes. One of these surveys was completely blank. Ten manager/supervisor survey responses were received that did not match up with subordinate survey responses and three subordinate responses did not pair up with a manager/supervisor response. Subordinate survey packages were filled out by seven of the Engineering Managers. Manager/supervisor and subordinate survey responses were paired up for 80 subordinates which is 81 percent of the Engineering Department.

Of the 80 paired survey responses, six had to be rejected because minimum KAI acceptance standards were not met. One of the six paired survey responses was rejected because the respondent failed to answer four of the 32 KAI survey questions. Five of the six paired survey responses, from Lab Technicians, were rejected for too many "Very Easy" responses. Some of the KAI responses are reverse coded so there must be a mix of "Very Easy" and "Very Hard" responses to be consistent. The most blatant KAI innovation survey response had all 33 responses in the "Very Easy" column. According to Kirton (1987), such a response turns up no more frequently than 1 in 100 and may come from an individual who is uneasy at work. The major technology changes taking place in the Test Lab at the time the surveys were administered could have been a factor in the high number of rejected KAI inventory surveys. The six rejected KAI inventory surveys lowered the number of paired survey responses to 74 or 75 percent of the Engineering Department.

DATA ANALYSIS

The first step in the data analysis of the research data was to create a data file that correctly represented the magnitude of all measured variables. This procedure was easy with the KAI innovation inventory because the reverse scored items are indicated on the inside page of the official questionnaire. The KAI is scored such that a higher score is more innovative. The (SO) score of the KAI is higher for increased idea generation. On the KAI the (E) score is higher when the respondent is less efficient. The KAI (R) score is higher for someone who dislikes a lot of rules.

The Leader-Member Exchange survey was scored such that a higher score represents a stronger relationship with supervisor. None of the Leader-Member Exchange questions were reverse scored. Work environment for innovation was assessed with 22 survey questions of which 16 measured support for innovation and 6 measured resource supply. Nine of the 16 support for innovation work environment survey questions were reverse scored. Two of the six work environment resource supply questions were reverse scored. None of the six survey questions on the Manager/Supervisor rating of subordinate innovative were reverse scored. A high innovative score represented a highly innovative individual. The survey role expectation question evaluated by each manager/supervisor for each subordinate was reversed scored with role requires an innovator as a one. The role expectation score was reversed in the research data base such that higher innovator expectations had a higher score than role requires a supporter. The KAI (SO), (E), and (R) scores were multiplied by 32/13, 32/7, and 32/12 respectively to provide a total KAI equivalent score. The KAI efficiency bias measure was the equivalent (SO) and (R) scores averaged minus the equivalent (E) score.

The path model in Figure 1 of Chapter 1 was evaluated using structural equation modeling. Structural equation modeling is an extension of several multivariate techniques, mainly multiple regression and factor analysis (Hair, Anderson, Tatham, & Black 1992). Structural equation modeling has been used in many fields including education, marketing, psychology, sociology, management, testing and measurement, health, demography, organizational behavior, biology, and genetics (Hair, Anderson, Tatham, & Black 1992). According to Hair, Anderson, Tatham, and Black (1992) structural equation modeling is twofold. First, structural equation modeling provides a straightforward method of dealing with multiple relationships simultaneously. Second, structural equation modeling with its ability to assess the relationships comprehensively provides a transition from exploratory to confirmatory analysis.

An example of research using structural equation modeling is the research by Scott and Bruce (1994) on the determinants of individual innovative behavior. They used a version of structural equation modeling called LISREL VI to evaluate their research. Scott and Bruce (1994) used structural equation modeling to assess a traditional path model, like the one in Figure 1, by estimating paths simultaneously. They were also able to obtain a goodness-of-fit index for their model by removing non-significant paths and increasing degrees of freedom. A newer windows version of LISREL VI called Amos 3.6 for Windows was used to evaluate this research data.

The data was also evaluated using more traditional statistical methods such as correlation analysis and multiple linear regression. Structural equation modeling has an absolute minimum sample size of 50 with a preferred sample size of 100 to 200 (Hair, Anderson, Tatham & Black 1992). The research sample in this research is composed of 34 Product Engineers, 8 Application Engineers, 7 Management Engineers, 18 Lab Technicians, and 14 Product Designers for a grand total of 81. The 7 managers are removed from the base sample because their Manager/Supervisor survey was not received. This left a base sample of 74 to evaluate the path diagram in Figure 1 using structural equation modeling. The six hypotheses proposed in this research are evaluated using structural equation modeling and multiple linear regression. Multiple linear regression was used to evaluate how the research variable relate to innovative behavior in the various work groups.

SUMMARY

Research questionnaires were administered at a high technology product development company to generate test data. This test data was used to evaluate the innovative behavior path diagram in Figure 1 and evaluate the six null hypotheses listed in this chapter. The research sample includes Product Development Engineers, Application Engineers, Management Engineers, Lab Technicians and Product Designers. Several established measures were used in this research to evaluate problem solving style, leadership, climate for innovation, role expectation and innovative behavior. The influence that problem solving style, leadership, climate for innovation, and role expectation have on individual innovative behavior was evaluated using structural equation modeling, correlation analysis, and multiple linear regression. Analytical results of the detailed analysis of this research data are presented in Chapter 4.

Analysis and Presentation of Findings

INTRODUCTION

In this chapter the analytical methods used to evaluate the research data and the findings are presented. The research data was first evaluated by reviewing means, standard deviations, minimum values, and maximum values for all research variables. A correlation matrix was created to evaluate the correlation of research variables. The base sample of 74 Engineering Department employees was evaluated using structural equation modeling techniques. The base sample was broken down into the four subgroups of 34 Product Engineers, 8 Application Engineers, 18 Lab Technicians and 14 Product Designers. A fifth subgroup was formed with seven Engineering Managers who filled out a subordinate survey package. Each of the subgroups was evaluated using multiple linear regression techniques. Structural equation modeling path estimates and regression coefficients were used to evaluate the rejection of the six null hypotheses. A seventh null hypothesis is presented and tested.

RESEARCH DATA EVALUATION

There were thirteen research variables measured or recorded for each of the 74 subordinates in the base research sample. The base sample contained Product Engineers, Application and Support Engineers, Lab Technicians, and Product Designers. For the base sample, the variable names, means, standard deviations, minimum values, and maximum values are listed in Table 4. This research sample was broken down into four groups. Table 5 lists the means, standard deviations, minimum values, and maximum values for the 34 Product Engineers included in the base sample. In Table 6 the means, standard deviations, minimum values, and maximum values for the 8 Application and Technical Support Engineers are listed. Table 7 and Table 8 include the means, standard deviations, minimum values, and maximum values for the Lab Technicians and Product Designers, respectively.

Table 4. Mean, Standard Deviations, and Ranges for the Base Sample of 34 Product Engineers, 8 Application Engineers, 18 Lab Technicians, and 14 Product Designers

Variables	Mean	Std Dev	Minimum	Maximum
1. Innovative behavior	16.65	6.14	6.00	29.00
2. Department	3.30	1.73	1.00	5.00
3. Education level	3.47	1.20	1.00	6.00
4. Age	40.45	11.10	21.00	65.00
5. Leader expectations	3.31	1.36	1.00	5.00
6. KAI score	98.86	12.89	60.00	141.00
7. Support for innovation	45.59	9.04	27.00	63.00
8. Resource supply	15.19	3.51	7.00	24.00
9. Leader-member exchange	48.57	10.25	22.00	68.00
10. KAI (SO)	114.33	16.35	71.40	155.10
11. KAI (E)	76.17	19.41	45.70	146.30
12. KAI (R)	95.35	17.93	56.00	149.30
13. KAI Efficiency Bias	28.67	21.81	-38.50	82.80

Note: N = 74.

Table 5. Mean, Standard Deviations, and Ranges for 34 Product Engineers

Variables	Mean	Std Dev	Minimum	Maximum
1. Innovative behavior	19.21	4.66	11.00	28.00
2. Department	5.00	0.00	5.00	5.00
3. Education level	4.35	0.85	2.00	6.00
4. Age	41.03	10.08	24.00	65.00
5. Leader expectations	3.85	0.99	1.00	5.00
6. KAI score	103.76	13.13	82.00	141.00
7. Support for innovation	48.12	8.72	32.00	63.00
8. Resource supply	13.82	3.94	7.00	24.00
9. Leader-member exchange	52.94	8.68	35.00	68.00
10. KAI (SO)	115.33	17.62	81.20	155.10
11. KAI (E)	84.17	21.03	45.70	146.30
12. KAI (R)	102.67	18.11	69.30	149.30
13. KAI Efficiency Bias	24.83	25.84	-38.50	82.80

Note: N = 34.

Table 6. Mean, Standard Deviations, and Ranges for 8 Application Engineers

Variables	Mean	Std Dev	Minimum	Maximum
1. Innovative behavior	21.25	6.54	11.00	29.00
2. Department	3.50	0.53	3.00	4.00
3. Education level	3.75	0.71	2.00	4.00
4. Age	37.63	15.30	23.00	61.00
5. Leader expectations	4.25	0.46	4.00	5.00
6. KAI score	101.50	9.45	88.00	114.00
7. Support for innovation	46.88	8.89	33.00	57.00
8. Resource supply	14.75	1.39	12.00	16.00
9. Leader-member exchange	54.25	8.71	40.00	66.00
10. KAI (SO)	122.77	13.12	100.90	145.20
11. KAI (E)	76.00	14.65	54.90	96.00
12. KAI (R)	93.33	15.29	74.70	117.30
13. KAI Efficiency Bias	32.05	19.03	-8.20	46.00

Note: N = 8.

Table 7. Mean, Standard Deviations, and Ranges for 18 Lab Technicians

Variables	Mean	Std Dev	Minimum	Maximum
1. Innovative behavior	12.56	5.95	6.00	26.00
2. Department	1.00	0.00	1.00	1.00
3. Education level	2.61	0.70	1.00	4.00
4. Age	39.44	10.59	21.00	58.00
5. Leader expectations	1.56	1.04	1.00	4.00
6. KAI score	94.22	13.02	60.00	119.00
7. Support for innovation	43.67	8.18	32.00	59.00
8. Resource supply	17.11	3.05	12.00	22.00
9. Leader-member exchange	42.28	7.38	30.00	54.00
10. KAI (SO)	112.82	16.53	71.40	142.80
11. KAI (E)	69.84	15.43	45.70	114.30
12. KAI (R)	88.30	16.02	56.00	117.30
13. KAI Efficiency Bias	30.72	17.53	-2.00	67.20

Note: N = 18.

Table 8. Mean, Standard Deviations, and Ranges for 14 Product Designers

Variables	Mean	Std Dev	Minimum	Maximum
1. Innovative behavior	13.07	4.50	6.00	20.00
2. Department	2.00	0.00	2.00	2.00
3. Education level	2.29	0.83	1.00	4.00
4. Age	41.93	12.34	27.00	63.00
5. Leader expectations	3.71	0.83	1.00	4.00
6. KAI score	91.43	8.27	75.00	103.00
7. Support for innovation	41.21	9.63	27.00	61.00
8. Resource supply	16.29	2.30	13.00	20.00
9. Leader-member exchange	42.79	11.24	22.00	61.00
10. KAI (SO)	109.01	13.57	78.80	125.50
11. KAI (E)	64.98	14.48	45.70	100.60
12. KAI (R)	87.81	15.42	61.30	112.00
13. KAI Efficiency Bias	33.43	17.40	3.00	66.00

Note: N = 14.

The means, standard deviations, minimum values, and maximum values for the 7 Engineering Managers are listed in Table 9. Note that values for innovative behavior and leader expectations are not available for Management Engineers. This is because a Manager's survey evaluation of these variables was not received. For this reason the seven managers were not included in the base research sample of 74. Another member of Engineering Management was asked to force rank the seven Engineering Managers, Product Engineers, Application Engineers, Support Engineers, Lab Technicians, and Product Designers from most to least innovative. This force rank order was later used to evaluate the determinants of innovative behavior of the Engineering Manager sample with multiple linear regression.

Table 10 contains the bivariate correlations for the 13 variables in the base sample using the Pearson Product-Moment. The variables Department, Education level, Leader expectations, KAI Score, Leader-member exchange, KAI (E), and KAI (R) are all significantly positively correlated with Innovative behavior, Resource supply was significantly negatively correlated with innovative behavior. The correlation matrix gives support for rejecting null hypotheses 1, 3, 4, and 5. No support was given in the correlation matrix for rejecting null hypotheses 2 or 6 with the base sample. The null hypotheses were further tested using structural equation modeling and multiple linear regression.

Table 9. Mean, Standard Deviations, and Ranges for 7 Management Engineers. *No Manager/Supervisor surveys were received for these individuals so rows 1 and 5 are blank.*

Variables	Mean	Std Dev	Minimum	Maximum
1. Innovative behavior	n/a	n/a	n/a	n/a
2. Department	6.00	0.00	6.00	6.00
3. Education level	4.43	0.53	4.00	5.00
4. Age	46.71	8.92	37.00	61.00
5. Leader expectations	n/a	n/a	n/a	n/a
6. KAI score	106.14	12.10	83.00	121.00
7. Support for innovation	53.29	10.63	39.00	66.00
8. Resource supply	15.00	5.03	7.00	21.00
9. Leader-member exchange	54.43	4.12	46.00	59.00
10. KAI (SO)	127.30	10.61	115.70	147.70
11. KAI (E)	77.71	24.90	32.00	105.10
12. KAI (R)	99.81	14.99	72.00	122.70
13. KAI Efficiency Bias	35.84	19.69	2.00	64.30

Note: N = 7.

Table 10. Bivariate Correlations for Research Variables in the Base Sample Using Pearson Product-Moment

Variables	1	2	3	4	5	6	7
1. Innovative behavior	—	.526	.400	.062	.522	.292	.071
	—	.000	.000	.299	.000	.006	.275
2. Department		—	.711	.032	.574	.374	.287
		—	.000	.393	.000	.001	.007
3. Education level			—	-.113	.396	.357	.194
			—	.169	.000	.001	.049
4. Age				—	-.155	-.135	.169
				—	.094	.125	.075
5. Leader expectations					—	.183	.025
					—	.059	.417
6. KAI score						—	.022
						—	.426
7. Support for innovation							—
							—
8. Resource supply							
9. Leader-member exchange							
10. KAI (SO)							
11. KAI (E)							
12. KAI (R)							
13. KAI Efficiency Bias							

Note: The top number is variable correlation and the bottom number is the one-tailed significance level.

N = 74

Table 10. (*Cont.*)

Variables	8	9	10	11	12	13
1. Innovative behavior	-.369	.258	.118	.239	.292	-.048
	.001	.013	.158	.020	.006	.343
2. Department	-.396	.501	.105	.380	.373	-.146
	.000	.000	.187	.000	.001	.107
3. Education level	-.312	.339	.113	.320	.371	-.091
	.003	.002	.169	.003	.001	.221
4. Age	.049	-.033	-.183	-.038	-.055	-.057
	.339	.391	.060	.374	.322	.315
5. Leader expectations	-.204	.227	-.026	.205	.247	-.091
	.041	.026	.413	.040	.017	.221
6. KAI score	-.333	.172	.745	.500	.864	.189
	.002	.071	.000	.000	.000	.053
7. Support for innovation	.397	.337	-.042	.168	-.022	-.175
	.000	.002	.362	.076	.425	.069
8. Resource supply	—	-.135	-.176	-.114	-.393	-.126
	—	.127	.067	.167	.000	.143
9. Leader-member exchange		—	.156	.088	.121	.030
		—	.093	.229	.152	.399
10. KAI (SO)			—	-.012	.448	.569
			—	.461	.000	.000
11. KAI (E)				—	.339	-.755
				—	.002	.000
12. KAI (R)					—	.277
					—	.008
13. KAI Efficiency Bias						—
						—

Note: The top number is variable correlation and the bottom number is the one-tailed significance level. N = 74

STRUCTURAL EQUATION MODEL

The base sample raw data was transferred directly from a SPSS data file into the AMOS 3.6 Structural Equation Modeling program. Earlier versions of structural equation modeling software such as LISREL VI, required the researcher to enter either a correlation or covariance matrix. A structural equation model like the one in Figure 2 with additional paths was entered. All the exogenous variables were allow to covary in the structural equation model. A latent error variable was pathed to each of the three endogenous variables. The regression weight for the path between the three endogenous variables and the latent error variables was set to a value of one. This is consistent with recommendations by Arbuckle (1997).

The strategy in evaluating the path diagram in Figure 1 using structural equation modeling was to start with a just identified model. This is when the degrees of freedom in the model are equal to zero. The least significant paths were removed one or two at a time and the structural equation model was reevaluated. Each path removed added one degree of freedom to the model. This iterative process continued until a balance between degrees of freedom and model fit was achieved. The final version of the structural equation model with variables KAI and KAI Efficiency Bias is shown in Figure 2.

In terms of goodness-of-fit indicators, the model in Figure 2 accounted for 42 percent of the variance in innovative behavior. The model accounted for 46 percent and 20 percent of the variance of the other two endogenous variables support for innovation and resource supply respectively. The structural equation model for the Scott and Bruce (1994) research accounted for 37 percent, 39 percent, and 29 percent of the variance for innovative behavior, support for innovation, and resource supply respectively. An excellent fit for the model was obtained with a Chi-square value of 3.46, 8 degrees of freedom, and a probability value of 0.90. The goodness of fit indicator value was 0.99 and the adjusted goodness of fit indicator value was 0.94.

A similar iterative structural equation modeling process was completed with the three KAI component variables KAI (SO), KAI (E), and KAI (R) in place of KAI and KAI Efficiency Bias variables. This final structural equation modeling path diagram is shown in Figure 3. In terms of goodness-of-fit indicators, the model in Figure 3 accounted for 43 percent of the variance in innovative behavior. The model accounted for 46 percent and 24 percent of the variance of the other two endogenous vari-

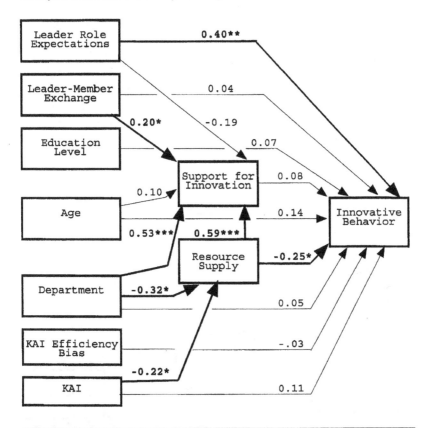

Figure 2. Structural equation modeling path model for base research sample of 74 Engineers, Designers, and Technicians with KAI.

Estimated path significance: *p < 0.05; **p < 0.01; ***p < 0.001

ables support for innovation and resource supply respectively. An even better fit was obtained for this structural equation model with a Chi-square value of 1.94, 9 degrees of freedom, and a probability value of 0.99. The goodness of fit indicator had a value of 0.99 and the adjusted goodness of fit indicator had a value of 0.97.

The significance level of the regression weights calculated were evaluated using the structural equation modeling critical ratio. The critical ratio is the regression weight estimate divided by the estimated standard error. This statistic is similar to the t-statistic but is only an approximation because structural equation modeling estimates the standard error term (Arbuckle, 1997). The critical ratio was used to approximate the t-statistic significance of regression coefficients. Regression coefficients that are significant for a one-tailed significance are listed in bold type in Figure 2 and Figure 3. Listed in Table 11 are the standardized structural equation modeling path estimates and associated critical ratios.

Several significant structural equation path estimates were determined. For the models with KAI and KAI factors seven significant path estimates were determined for each. Five of the significant paths were positive and two were negative. The structural equation model supports re-

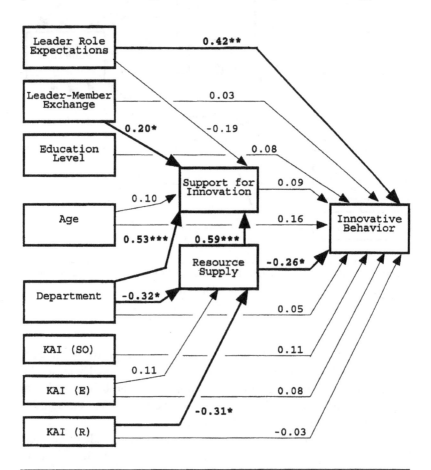

Figure 3. Structural equation modeling path model for base research sample of 74 Engineers, Designers, and Technicians with KAI components.
Estimated path significance: *p < 0.05; **p < 0.01; ***p < 0.001

jection on Null Hypothesis 4 and Null Hypothesis 5 at the 0.05 and 0.001 significance levels respectively. There was support for Hypothesis 1, but the level of significance was not sufficient to reject the Null Hypothesis 1 at the 0.05 significance level. Little or no support was found for the rejection of Null Hypotheses 2, 3, or 6 with the base sample.

Variables other than the ones originally hypothesized had significant path estimates in the structural equation model. The path coefficient between Resource supply and innovative behavior was negative at the 0.05 significance level. The variables department and resource supply both had a positive path coefficient to support for innovation at the 0.001 significance level. Variables Department and KAI had a negative path coefficient to resource supply at the 0.05 significance level. In the second structural equation model with KAI factors the KAI (R) factor replaced KAI with a negative path coefficient to resource supply at the 0.05 significance level. The critical ratio was greater for KAI (R) than for the general KAI score. Breaking down the KAI score into the three factors of (SO), (E), and (R) gives the researcher more insight into the significance of each KAI factor. For these reasons the structural equation path model with KAI factors was more informative than the path model with the combined KAI score only.

Table 11. Standardized Structural Equation Modeling Path Estimates with Estimated Significance Level for Base Sample

Path Variable	Dependent Variable	Path Model With KAI	Path Model With KAI Factors
Leader Role Expectations	Innovative	0.400**	0.416**
	Behavior	3.476	3.579
Leader-Member Exchange	Innovative	0.042	0.031
	Behavior	0.386	0.287
Education Level	Innovative	0.071	0.082
	Behavior	0.542	0.630
Age	Innovative	0.142	0.155
	Behavior	1.489	1.602
Department	Innovative	0.054	0.048
	Behavior	0.301	0.266
KAI	Innovative	1.106	——
	Behavior	1.015	

Table 11. (*cont.*)

Path Variable	Dependent Variable	Path Model with KAI	Path Model with KAI Factors
KAI Efficiency Bias	Innovative Behavior	-0.027 -0.281	——
KAI (SO)	Innovative Behavior	——	0.111 1.047
KAI (E)	Innovative Behavior	——	0.078 1.770
KAI (R)	Innovative Behavior	——	-0.032 -0.272
Support for Innovation	Innovative Behavior	0.083 0.686	0.087 0.725
Resource Supply	Innovative Behavior	-0.245* -2.000	-0.260* -2.097
Leader Role Expectations	Support for Innovation	-0.186 -1.717	-0.186 -1.717
Leader-Member Exchange	Support for Innovation	0.201* 2.003	0.201* 2.002
Age	Support for Innovation	0.102 1.145	0.101 1.146
Department	Support for Innovation	0.526*** 4.142	0.525*** 4.159
Resource Supply	Support for Innovation	0.592*** 6.290	0.591*** 6.293
Department	Resource Supply	-0.316* -2.791	-0.324* -2.810
KAI	Resource Supply	-0.215* -1.902	——
KAI (E)	Resource Supply	——	0.114 1.007
KAI (R)	Resource Supply	——	-0.311* -2.747

Note: The top number is standardized structural equation modeling path estimate and the bottom number is critical "ratio." * $p < 0.05$, ** $p < 0.01$, ***$p < 0.001$

MULTIPLE LINEAR REGRESSION OF RESEARCH DATA

Multiple linear regression was used to investigate the determinants of innovative behavior in the various sup-groups in the Engineering Department of XYZ Company. Structural equation modeling could not be used because the minimum sample size recommended is 50 (Hair, Anderson, Tatham & Black 1992). The three KAI factors were used in place of the combined KAI score in most of the regression analyses. Regression analyses were performed on six group samples. The six group samples are the base sample, Product Engineers, Application Engineers, Management Engineers, Lab Technicians, and Product Designers. Results of the regression analyses for innovative behavior, support for innovation and resource supply are listed in Table 12, Table 13, and Table 14 respectively. Each regression analysis was started with all variables being regressed with the dependent variable. The less significant variables were removed in an attempt to increase the regression analysis F Statistic significance.

Base Sample

The regression analysis for the base sample of 74 with research variables and the three dependent variables innovative behavior, support for innovation, and resource supply all had a F statistic that was significant at the 0.001 level. Regression analysis results of the base sample variables with innovative behavior were similar to the structural equation modeling results. Leader role expectation was found to have a positive regression coefficient with a one-tailed significance level of 0.001. The Resource supply regression coefficient was negative with a one-tailed significance level of 0.05. When the variables were regressed with support for innovation the positive significant paths were with the variables department and resource supply like the structural equation model. The regression coefficient for leader-member exchange was found to be positive but not significant like the structural equation model.

Table 12. Results of Regression Analysis for Subgroup Variables With Innovative Behavior

Variables	Base Sample N=74	Product Eng. N=34	Appl. Eng. N=8	Manag. Eng. N=7	Lab N=18	Design N=14
Department	—	—	—	—	—	—
Education level	0.12	0.24	-0.28 *	-0.42 *	—	-0.42
Age	0.15	0.23	0.93 *	—	0.40	—
Leader role expectations	0.44 ***	0.39 *	—	n/a	0.62 *	—
KAI	—	—	—	0.49 *	—	—
Support for innovation	0.13	-0.36 *	0.42 *	-0.69 **	—	—
Resource supply	-0.28 *	—	—	—	-0.87 **	-0.90 *
Leader-member exchange	—	-0.42 **	—	-0.64 **	0.67 *	—
KAI (SO)	0.10	0.33 *	—	0.72 **	0.41	—
KAI (E)	—	—	—	—	—	—
KAI (R)	—	—	-0.20 *	—	-0.56 *	—
KAI Efficiency Bias	—	—	0.59 *	—	-0.71 *	—
Adjusted R sq	0.359	0.359	0.998	0.999	0.485	0.457
F	7.82 ***	4.08 **	989 *	7523 **	3.669 *	4.62 *

Note: Base Sample contains survey results from 34 Product Engineers, 8 Application Engineers, 18 Lab Technicians, and 14 Product Designers. The "Appl. Eng." column is for Application Engineers. The "Manag. Eng." column is for Engineering Managers who filled out a subordinate survey package. All variables were regressed against survey variable innovative behavior except Managers and Lab Technicians which were regressed against rank order innovative behavior. The significance levels are noted as follows: * $p < 0.05$; ** $p < 0.01$; *** $p < 0.001$.

Table 13. Results of Regression Analysis for Subgroup Variables With Support for Innovation

Variables	Base Sample N=74	Product Eng. N=34	Appl. Eng. N=8	Manag. Eng. N=7	Lab N=18	Design N=14
Department	0.52 ***	—	0.68 **	—	—	—
Education level	—	—	—	—	—	-0.81 *
Age	0.10	—	—	1.44 *	-0.10	—
Leader role expectations	-0.19	—	—	n/a	0.21	-0.70 **
KAI	—	—	—	—	—	—
Support for innovation	—	—	—	—	—	—
Resource supply	0.59 ***	0.57 ***	0.87 **	-0.93 *	0.61 ***	-0.69
Leader-member exchange	0.20	—	-0.80 **	—	0.57 **	—
KAI (SO)	—	—	—	-0.93 *	0.16	—
KAI (E)	—	—	—	-0.73	—	—
KAI (R)	—	—	—	1.09 *	—	-0.43
KAI Efficiency Bias	—	—	—	—	—	—
Adjusted R sq	0.423	0.310	0.935	0.995	0.77	0.70
F	11.72 ***	15.85 ***	34.48 **	256.9 *	12.42 ***	8.61 **

Note: Base Sample contains survey results from 34 Product Engineers, 8 Application Engineers, 18 Lab Technicians, and 14 Product Designers. The "Appl. Eng." column is for Application Engineers. The "Manag. Eng." column is for Engineering Managers who filled out a subordinate survey package. All variables were regressed against survey variable Support For Innovation.

The significance levels are noted as follows: * $p < 0.05$; ** $p < 0.01$; *** $p < 0.001$.

Table 14. Results of Regression Analysis for Subgroup Variables With Resource Supply

Variables	Base Sample N=74	Product Eng. N=34	Appl. Eng. N=8	Manag. Eng. N=7	Lab N=18	Design N=14
Department	-0.55 ***	—		—	—	—
Education level	—	—	—	—	—	-0.68 ***
Age	—	—	-0.49 *	1.54 *	0.21	—
Leader role expectations	0.16		—	n/a	—	—
KAI	—	—	—	—	—	—
Support for innovation	0.56 ***	0.54 ***	0.72 *	-1.07 *	0.79 **	—
Resource supply	—	—	—	—	—	—
Leader-member exchange	-0.06	—	—	—	-0.12 *	-0.16
KAI (SO)		—	—	-0.99 *	—	—
KAI (E)	0.05	—	—	-0.78 *	0.43 *	—
KAI (R)	-.22 *	-0.23	0.23	1.17 *	-0.28	-0.54 **
KAI Efficiency Bias	—	—	—	—	—	—
Adjusted R sq	0.453	0.345	0.83	0.995	0.711	0.734
F	11.09 ***	9.68 ***	12.3 *	225 *	9.379 ***	12.97 ***

Note: Base Sample contains survey results from 34 Product Engineers, 8 Application Engineers, 18 Lab Technicians, and 14 Product Designers. The "Appl. Eng." column is for Application Engineers. The "Manag. Eng." column is for Engineering Managers who filled out a subordinate survey package. All variables were regressed against survey variable Resource Supply.
The significance levels are noted as follows: * $p < 0.05$; ** $p < 0.01$; *** $p < 0.001$.

Table 14 lists the regression analysis results for variables regressed with resource supply. Like in the structural equation model the variables department and KAI (R) both had a negative correlation coefficient with 0.001 and 0.05 significance levels respectively. Unlike the structural equation model the regression model indicated a significant regression coefficient with variable support for innovation. The reason for this is the way structural equation modeling evaluates the complete model simultaneously. Regression analysis results supported the rejection of Null Hypothesis 5 only with the base sample.

The regression results for the various subgroups were not consistent with the regression results of the base sample. Listed in Table 12, Table 13 and Table 14 are the regression coefficients and significance levels for variables regressed with the dependent variables innovative behavior, Support for innovation, and resource supply respectively. The positive regression coefficient for the base sample between leader role expectation and innovative behavior appears to be driven by Product Engineers and Lab Technicians. Lab Technicians and Product Designers appear to have driven the negative regression coefficient between resource supply and innovative behavior in the base sample. The various Engineering sub-groups may have canceled out trends in base sample regression analysis. The regression analysis of the various Engineering Department groups is evaluated next.

Product Engineers The regression analysis for the Product Engineer sample of 34 engineers with the independent variables and the research variables innovative behavior, support for innovation, and resource supply had an F statistic that was significant at the 0.01, 0.001, and 0.001 levels respectively. There were four regression coefficients with innovative behavior that were significant by at least the 0.05 level. Leader role expectation had a positive regression coefficient with innovative behavior at the 0.05 level which supports rejection of Null Hypothesis 5 for this group. KAI (SO) had a positive regression coefficient with innovative behavior at the 0.05 level. The regression coefficient was not significant when KAI (SO) was replaced with the combined KAI score. Leader-member exchange had a negative correlation coefficient with innovative behavior at the 0.001 significance level which does not support the rejection of Null Hypothesis 3. Support for innovation had a negative correlation coefficient with innovative behavior at the 0.05 significance level which does not support the rejection of Null Hypothesis 6. Regression analysis gave support for the rejection of Null Hypothesis 5 only with the Product Engineer Subgroup.

Application Engineers In the Application Engineer regression analysis with innovative behavior five variables were found to have significant regression coefficients. Support was found for the rejection of Null Hypothesis 6 with a positive regression coefficient between support for innovation and innovative behavior at the .05 significance level. Support was also found for the rejection of Null Hypothesis 2 with a positive regression coefficient between KAI efficiency bias and innovative behavior at the 0.05 significance level. The Application Engineer subgroup is the only sample in this research that supports rejection of Null Hypothesis 2 and Null Hypothesis 6. Age had a positive regression coefficient with innovative behavior at the 0.05 significance level. Both education level and KAI (R) had a negative regression coefficient with innovative behavior at the 0.05 significance level. Regression analysis gave support for the rejection of Null Hypothesis 2 and Null Hypothesis 6 only with the Application Engineer Subgroup.

Management Engineers The Management Engineering subgroup sample had five variables with significant regression coefficients with innovative behavior. Management Engineers like the Product Engineers had significant negative regression coefficients between support for innovation and leader-member exchange and the dependent variable innovative behavior. These are the only subgroups with these significant negative relationships that do not support the rejection of Null Hypothesis 3 or Null Hypothesis 6. The regression coefficient between KAI and innovative behavior was positive at the 0.05 significancy level. This significant relationship supports the rejection of Null Hypothesis 1. The regression coefficient between leader-member exchange and support for innovation was negative at the 0.01 significance level. This relationship is in the same direction as Null Hypothesis 4 and therefore does not support the rejection of this null hypothesis. Note that leader expectation was not measured for Management Engineers and the innovation level used for regression analysis was a force rank order by another member of Engineering Management.

Lab Technicians It was not possible to obtain an F statistic with a 0.05 or less significance level with the Lab Technician subgroup with the supervisor evaluated measure of innovative behavior level. Further investigation of the test data found discrepancies in the survey data. One Lab Technician supervisor with 11 subordinates had a mean innovative behavior score of 8.91 with a standard deviation of 2.17. Another Lab technician supervisor with 6 subordinates in this research gave a mean innovative behavior score of 19.5 with a standard deviation of 4.85. It is highly unlikely that the actual mean innovative behavior score of the two Lab Technician groups would be that vastly different. To evaluate the research data using regression analysis the force rank order innovative behavior ratings were used in place of the Manager/Supervisor evaluated innovative behavior.

The Lab Technician sample had five variables with significant regression coefficients. Support was found for the rejection of Null Hypothesis 3, Null Hypothesis 4, and Null Hypothesis 5 at the 0.05 significance level. Resource supply was found to have a negative regression coefficient with innovative behavior at the 0.01 significance level. The regression coefficient for KAI efficiency bias was negative with a 0.05 significance level.

Product Designers The Product Designer sample had only one variable with a significant regression coefficient with innovative behavior. Resource supply variable had a negative regression coefficient with innovative behavior at the 0.05 significance level. No support was found to reject any of the Null Hypotheses in this research for the Product Designer subgroup.

EVALUATION OF NULL HYPOTHESES

The subgroup regression coefficients varied greatly for the five subgroups. One subgroup would have a significantly positive regression coefficient while another may have a significantly negative regression coefficient for the same variables. Support was found for the rejection of all six null hypothesis in at least one subgroup. The support of the rejection of the six null hypotheses is reviewed next.

Null Hypothesis 1 is as follows: the degree to which an individual's problem solving style is innovative is either negatively related or not related to his or her innovative behavior. The only support found in this research for rejection of Null Hypothesis 1 was in the regression analysis for the Management Engineer subgroup. When the KAI score was broken down into the three components (SO), (E), and (R) the (SO) component had a significant positive regression coefficient with both The Project Engineering and the Management Engineering subgroups.

Null Hypothesis 2 is as follows: The degree to which an individual's KAI efficiency bias is positive is either negatively related or not related to his or her innovative behavior. The only support found for rejecting Null Hypothesis 2 was the Application Engineering subgroup. The Lab Technician subgroup had a significantly negative regression coefficient for Null Hypothesis 2.

Null Hypothesis 3 is as follows: The quality of the leader-member exchange between an individual and his or her supervisor is either negatively related or not related to the individual's innovative behavior. The only support found for the rejection of Null Hypothesis 2 was with the Lab Technician subgroup where the regression coefficient was significant at the 0.05 level. Both the Product Engineering and Management Engineering subgroups had negative regression coefficients at the 0.01 significant level for Null Hypothesis 3.

Null Hypothesis 4 is as follows: The quality of leader-member exchange between an individual and his or her supervisor is either negatively related or not related to the degree to which the individual perceives dimensions of climate as supportive of innovation. Rejection of Null Hypothesis 4 was supported for the Lab Technician subgroup. The regression coefficient was significant at the 0.01 level. Support for rejection of Null Hypothesis 4 was also found in the structural equation modeling analysis of the base sample where significance was estimated at the 0.05 level. The regression coefficient for Application Engineers was negative at the 0.001 significance level for Null Hypothesis 4.

Null Hypothesis 5 is as follows: The degree to which a supervisor expects a subordinate to be innovative is either negatively related or not related to subordinates' innovative behavior. Support for the rejection of Null Hypothesis 5 was found in both the regression analysis and the structural equation model for the base sample with 0.001 and 0.01 significance levels respectively. The regression analysis for both the Product Engineer and Lab Technician subgroup supports rejection of Null Hypothesis 5 at the 0.05 significance level.

Null Hypothesis 6 is as follows: The degree to which individuals perceive dimensions of organizational climate as supportive of innovation is either negatively related or not related to their innovative behavior. The only support found for rejecting Null Hypothesis 6 was the Application Engineering subgroup. The regression coefficient significance level was 0.05. The regression coefficient for Null Hypothesis 6 was negative for the Product Engineering and Management Engineering subgroups with 0.05 and 0.01 levels of significance respectively.

ADDITIONAL ANALYSIS OF RESEARCH DATA

The KAI efficiency bias was further analyzed with the additional Null Hypothesis 7. Null Hypotheses 7 is as follows: The KAI efficiency bias is negative or equal to zero for all population samples. For the base sample of 74 participants the KAI efficiency bias mean was 28.67 with a standard deviation of 21.81. With a test value of zero the t-value was 11.31 with 73 degrees of freedom. Null Hypothesis 7 is rejected at the 0.0005 significance level in the one-tailed test for the base sample.

SUMMARY

In this chapter the evaluation of research data was reviewed. First, the means, standard deviations, minimum values and maximum values for all research variable results were evaluated. The base sample of 74 Engineering Department employees was further broken down into four subgroups. The subgroups were 34 Product Engineers, 8 Application Engineers, 18 Lab Technicians, and 14 Product Designers. An additional subgroup of 7 Engineering Managers was created with the Managers that filled out a subordinate survey package.

Structural equation modeling techniques were used to evaluate the proposed path model with the base sample. Additional analysis of the research data was performed on the base sample and the subgroups using linear regression analysis. The six null hypotheses were evaluated using the structural equation modeling results and the linear regression results. Support was found for rejecting each of the six null hypotheses in at least one Engineering Department subgroup. Additional analysis of the KAI efficiency bias was made by proposing Null Hypothesis 7. Strong support was found for the rejection of Null Hypothesis 7.

In Chapter 5 the researcher provides a discussion of the statistical results presented in this chapter. The implications of this research and directions for future research are also discussed.

Summary and Conclusions

INTRODUCTION

In this chapter the support for the rejection of seven null hypotheses is reviewed. The use of Kirton Adaption-Innovation theory, leader-member exchange theory, leader expectation theory, and organizational climate theory in this research is reviewed. The problems found in this research with the supervisor evaluated subordinate innovative behavior survey are reviewed with suggested solutions. The study limitations of this research and directions for future research are also reviewed.

NULL HYPOTHESES

Support was found for the rejection of all null hypothesis in at least one Engineering Department subgroup. The only support found in this research for rejection of Null Hypothesis 1 was in the regression analysis for the Management Engineer subgroup. The only support found for rejecting Null Hypothesis 2 was the Application Engineering subgroup. The only support found for the rejection of Null Hypothesis 3 was with the Lab Technician subgroup. The Rejection of Null Hypothesis 4 was supported by the regression analysis for the Lab Technician subgroup. Support for rejection of Null Hypothesis 4 was also found in the structural equation modeling analysis of the base sample. Support for the rejection of Null Hypothesis 5 was found in both the regression analysis and the structural equation model for the base sample. The regression analysis for both the Product Engineer and Lab Technician subgroups supports the rejection of Null Hypothesis 5. The only support found for rejecting Null Hypothesis 6 was the Application Engineering subgroup. Null Hypothesis 7 was rejected for the base sample.

KIRTON ADAPTION-INNOVATION THEORY AND INNOVATIVE BEHAVIOR

This research supports the Kirton Adaption-Innovation (KAI) Inventory as a useful instrument in measuring some of the determinants of individual innovative behavior. The KAI Inventory was found to be even more informative when the three KAI factors (SO), (E), and (R) were used in place of the total KAI score. In several of the subgroup regression analyses the regression coefficient was not significant with the KAI variable. But, when the KAI score was replaced with the three KAI factors one of the factors would often have a significant regression coefficient. The KAI factor sufficiency versus proliferation of originality (SO) had a positive regression coefficient with innovative behavior for both the Product Engineer and the Management Engineer subgroup. An individual with a higher (SO) score has a tendency to create more ideas than an individual with a lower (SO) score. In this research Project Engineers and Management Engineers with higher KAI (SO) scores were rated with higher levels of individual innovative behavior.

The KAI factor reliability and efficiency (E) did not have a significant regression coefficient with innovative behavior for any of the subgroups. The mean of the KAI efficiency bias factor was 28.67 for the base sample. The significance of this value is that participants in the base sample consistently had more adaptive (E) scores than averaged (SO) and (R) scores. The rejection of Null Hypothesis 7 also supports a KAI efficiency bias for the base sample. The findings of this research are contrary to Kirton, (personal communication, February 28, 1996) who said it is uncommon for the normalized KAI scores of the three factor groups to vary a great deal from each other for an individual on the adaption-innovation continuum. More research is needed to evaluate the KAI efficiency bias. It may be that the majority of Engineering Department employees in high technology product development organizations have a positive KAI efficiency bias.

The KAI factor rule/group conformity (R) had a significant negative regression coefficient with innovative behavior for both the Application Engineer and Lab Technician subgroup. An individual with a low KAI (R) score likes to work in an environment with more rules than an individual with a high KAI (R) score. The Application Engineers and the Lab Technicians were evaluated as more innovative if they had an adaptive orientation with the KAI rule/group conformity (R) factor. This was not the case for the other three subgroups which each had a nonsignificant regression coefficient between KAI (R) and innovative behavior.

The mean KAI score for the base sample was just above the average KAI score in the United States and United Kingdom of 95.5 with a value of 98.9. The Engineering Manager subgroup had the highest KAI mean score at 106.1 and the highest KAI efficiency bias mean score of 35.8. The Engineering Manager subgroup also had the highest KAI (SO) and (R) scores of the Engineering Department subgroups. This reflects the push by top management in XYZ Company to be more innovative by putting more innovative individuals in Engineering Management positions.

An individual with a high KAI score and a high KAI efficiency bias score, like the Engineering Manager subgroup, has the best of the KAI factor scores for innovation. An individual with a high innovative (SO) score proliferate ideas and compulsively toys with ideas (Kirton, 1987). Individuals with high innovative (R) scores value highly the development of their ideas and do not like to operate within rules, structures, and consensus (Kirton, 1987). An individual with a low adaptive (E) score has a preference for precision, reliability, efficiency, and thoroughness (Kirton, 1987). Without an adaptive (E) score an individual may not be able to complete or follow through with innovative ideas in a complex high technology environment.

To get a positive KAI efficiency bias score an individual must have innovative (SO) and (R) scores and an adaptive (E) score as just described. The innovative and adaptive scores here are as Kirton (1976) labeled the ends of the adaption innovation continuum. An individual with innovative (SO) and (R) scores and an adaptive (E) score is uncommon according to Kirton (personal communication, February 28, 1996). More research needs to be performed to determine if a positive KAI efficiency bias score is common in highly innovative people in high technology organizations.

LEADER-MEMBER EXCHANGE THEORY AND INNOVATIVE BEHAVIOR

Both the structural equation model and linear regression analysis did not indicate a relationship between the quality of leader-member exchange and innovative behavior for the base sample. The affect of leader-member exchange on innovative behavior was nullified by the significant positive and negative regression coefficients of the various subgroups. The regression coefficient between leader-member exchange and innovative behavior was significantly positive for the Lab Technician subgroup. This means that the Lab technicians who believe their relationship with their supervisor has high levels of support trust, and autonomy are more innovative. In other words the stronger the leader-member exchange the more innovative the Lab Technician was evaluated by force rank order.

The opposite relationship was found for Product Engineers and Management Engineers. Both had significant negative regression coefficients between leader-member exchange and innovative behavior. Those Product Engineers and Management Engineers who were evaluated as more innovative had weaker leader-member exchange scores. The members of these groups who were evaluated with higher levels on innovative behavior did not feel higher levels of support, trust and autonomy with their supervisor. In other words the Engineers evaluated as having lower levels of innovative behavior had stronger relationships with their supervisors. One explanation for this is that Engineers with higher levels of individual innovative behavior felt their supervisor were limiting their innovative potential. The KAI (R) factor mean was greater for the Engineering than the Technicians subgroup. An individual with a higher (R) score does not like to operate within rules, structure, and consensus which is what management often imposes. The mean KAI (R) for Product Engineers, Management Engineers, and Lab Technicians was 102.7, 99.8 and 88.3 respectively.

LEADER EXPECTATIONS AND INNOVATIVE BEHAVIOR

The relationship between leader role expectations and innovative behavior was significantly positive for the base sample in both the structural equation model and the regression analysis. Product Engineers and Lab Technicians were the only subgroups with significant positive regression coefficients between leader role expectations and innovative behavior. The regression coefficient for Management Engineers could not be evaluated because their manager did not complete the leader expectation survey. No relationship was found with regression analysis between leader role expectations and innovative behavior for Application Engineers and Product Designers. The Application Engineering subgroup had the highest mean score for leader role expectations of the subgroups with a value of 4.25 and a standard deviation of 0.46. The regression coefficient between leader role expectations and innovative behavior was non significant for the Application Engineer subgroup because the supervisors gave everyone about the same high role expectation score.

ORGANIZATIONAL CLIMATE AND
INNOVATIVE BEHAVIOR

The organizational climate measure was broken down into support for innovation and resource supply. The structural equation modeling path coefficient and the linear regression coefficient between support for innovation and innovative behavior was not significant in either analysis for the base sample. The regression coefficient for the Application Engineer subgroup between support for innovation and innovative behavior was significantly positive. The regression coefficient between support for innovation and innovative behavior was significantly negative for both the Product Engineering and Management Engineering subgroups. Of all the subgroups, the mean support for innovation scores were highest for the Product Engineering and Management Engineering subgroups. The negative regression coefficient between support for innovation and innovative behavior simply means that the Engineers rated as more innovative viewed the environment as less supportive for innovation than the less innovative Engineers.

One explanation for this negative relationship is that the more innovative Engineers believe they are being held back by limited support for innovation. The more innovative Engineers may be more naturally driven to be innovative and are more sensitive to limited support for innovation. It is unlikely that reducing support for innovation would increase innovative behavior as the negative correlation coefficient suggests.

Both the structural equation model and the regression analysis had a significant negative coefficients between resource supply and innovative behavior for the base sample. The Lab Technicians and Product Designers also had significant negative regression coefficients between resource supply and innovative behavior. The more innovative Lab Technicians and Product Designers rated resource supply as less adequate than the less innovative individuals.

The subgroup with the lowest mean score for resource supply was the Product Engineering subgroup. A significant regression coefficient was not found between resource supply and innovative behavior for any of the Engineering subgroups. A likely reason for this is that subordinates consistently gave low scores for resource supply questions on the research surveys. The mean score for the Product Engineers was 13.8 with a possible high and low score of 30 and 6 respectively. Actually, the mean score for resource supply was low for all the Engineering Department subgroups with the Lab Technician subgroup having the highest mean score of 17.1.

There are six questions on the work environment survey that was used to measure the subordinates perception of resource supply. Two of the survey questions are as follows: (14.) Assistance in developing new ideas is readily available; (15.) There are adequate resources devoted to innovation in this organization. Subordinates evaluated each question on a five point Likert type scale with one equal to strongly disagree and five equal to strongly agree. The Engineering Department base sample had a mean resource supply value of 15.2. This means that the average response by subordinates on the resource supply survey was in the middle at 2.5 on a 5 point scale. This resource supply value suggests that subordinates in XYZ Company see room for improvement in resource supply. High technology product development organizations are in a constant state of being harvested for profits and must balance cost with benefits. More information and research is required to evaluate the cost benefit of increased resource supply perception by subordinates.

When evaluating the results of the regression analysis for the subgroups one must remember that the resource supply values are the individual's perception of resource supply, not an actual objective measure of resource supply. More research is needed in other high technology product development organizations to better understand the relationship between resource supply, innovative behavior, and cost.

THE MEASUREMENT OF INDIVIDUAL INNOVATIVE BEHAVIOR

One of the weak points in this research is the measurement of individual innovative behavior. This research used a six question survey developed by Scott and Bruce (1994) to measure innovative behavior. This individual innovative behavior evaluation survey was evaluated by each or the subordinate's manager/supervisor. One problem with this survey is that all managers/supervisors do not evaluate subordinates' relative level of individual innovative behavior equally. An example of this was discovered with two supervisors of Lab Technicians in this research. One supervisor with 11 subordinates gave a mean innovative behavior score of 8.91 with a standard deviation of 2.17 while another supervisor with 6 subordinates gave a mean innovative behavior score of 19.5 with a standard deviation of 4.85. These results are suspect because it is highly unlikely that the actual mean score of the two Lab Technician groups would vary a great deal. Suspicions were confirmed when a member of

Engineering Management was asked to force rank all Lab Technicians from least innovative to most innovative. The force rank order of Lab technicians had more innovative and less innovative Lab Technicians distributed between the two groups as would be expected.

One method to increase the accuracy of the individual innovative behavior measurement may be to give supervisors examples of innovative behavior. An example of an individual with high, average, and low individual innovative behavior levels would help the supervisor evaluate their subordinates' individual innovative behavior rating to an established baseline. Another method would be to have a member of management, who is familiar with the individual innovative behavior of all subordinates, force rank order research participants from least to most innovative. For larger research groups it would be good to get several members of management to work together on the most appropriate force rank order of research participants. The force rank order of individual innovative behavior can be compared to the order of all participants ranked by the magnitude of their supervisor's innovative behavior rating. Use of these methods would establish a quick validity check of the innovative behavior rating of research participants.

A problem with the measurement of individual innovative behavior by subordinate supervisors is that the requirements for high individual innovative behavior can vary for each Engineering subgroup. Some example of this are given next. An Application Engineer may be considered innovative because he can be innovative when working out solutions with customers. A Product Design Engineer would be considered innovative if he is able to come up with new solutions that lead to new products and patents. Product Designers may be considered innovative if they come up with a more efficient way to design a part. Lab Technicians may be considered innovative if they come up with a way to solve an existing design problem. Engineering Managers may be considered innovative if they are able to solve personnel problems in new and different ways. It may not be correct to evaluate a Lab Technician and a Product Engineer with the same survey questionnaire and compare the results. Research needs to be performed with techniques such as force rank order on engineering subgroups to determine if the Scott and Bruce innovative behavior survey is a valid measure for comparison between engineering subgroups.

STUDY LIMITATIONS AND DIRECTIONS
FOR FUTURE RESEARCH

More research from other high technology product development organizations is needed to validate the findings of this research. In this research the relationships between individual problem solving style, leader-member exchange, support for innovation, resource supply, leader expectations, and individual innovative behavior was explored. Published research on the determinants of individual innovative behavior in high technology product development organizations is limited. This research is an extension of ground breaking research by Scott and Bruce (1994) on the determinants of individual innovative behavior in a research and development organization. This research is a first attempt to evaluate the determinants of innovative behavior in a high technology product development organization where cost and time constraints are more restrictive than in a research and development organization.

The determinants of innovative behavior were found to be different for various Engineering Department subgroups within the Engineering Department. A question to be answered by further research is, do other high technology product development organizations have the same determinants of individual innovative behavior in the various Engineering sup-groups as were found in this research? Future research sample sizes of 50 or more for each Engineering subgroup would help to strengthen and validate these research findings. Research samples with greater than 50 participants can be evaluated simultaneously using structural equation modeling techniques. Two other areas of particular interest for further research and study are the KAI efficiency bias on innovative behavior and the optimum level of resource supply for innovative behavior.

A better understanding of the determinants of individual innovative behavior in high technology product development organizations has many uses. This information can be used to further improve the level of innovation in an organization. A better understanding can be used to determine a cost effective level of support for innovation within Engineering subgroups. Knowledge gained from further research on innovative behavior can be used to more efficiently and effectively staff high technology product development organizations and special project teams. It may be possible with further research to guide new hires to the subgroup that best fits their strengths by evaluating a new hire survey.

Studying individual innovative behavior in a high technology product development organization is difficult for two reasons. First, the researcher must use perceptual measures to evaluate important research variables such as individual innovative behavior. Second, high technology product development organizations view innovation as a competitive tool and are reluctant to open up their organization to research on innovative behavior. The need for innovation research is great as companies face competitive, turbulent environments in which the ability to innovate could be the difference between success or failure.

Bibliography

Abbey, A., & Dickson, J. (1983). R&D work climate and innovation in semicon-ductors. *Academy of Management Journal.* Vol. 26, pp. 362-368.

Abernathy, W.J., & Utterback, J.M. (1978). Patterns of industrial innovation. *Technology Review*, Vol. 80 (June/July), pp. 41-47.

Amabile, T. (1988). A model of creativity and innovation in organizations. In B. M. Staw & L. L. Cummings (Eds.), *Research in organizational behavior*, Vol. 10, pp. 123-167. Greenwich, CT: JAI Press.

Amabile, T., & Gryskiewicz, N. (1989). The creative environment scales: The Work Environment Inventory. *Creativity Research Journal*, Vol. 2, pp. 231-254.

Ancona, D., & Caldwell, D. (1987). Management issues facing new product teams in high technology companies. In D. Lewin, D. Lipsky, & D. Sokel (Eds.), *Advances in industrial and labor relations*, Vol. 4, pp. 191-221. Greenwich, CT: JAI Press.

Angle, H. (1989). Psychology and organizational innovation. In A. Van de Ven, H. Angle, & M. Poole (Eds.), *Research on the management of innovation: The Minnesota studies*, pp. 135-170. New York: Harper & Row.

Arbuckle, James L. (1997). *Amos Users' Guide Version 3.6* Chicago: Small-Waters Corporation.

Bandura, A. (1988). Self-regulation of motivation and action through goal sys-tems. In V. Hamilton, F.H. Bower, & N.H. Frijda (Eds.), *Cognitive perspec-tives on emotion and motivation*, pp. 37-61. Dordrecht, Netherlands: Kluwer Academic Publishers.

Cohn, S.F. & Turyn, R.M. (1984). Organizational structure, decision-making procedures, and the adoption of innovations. *IEEE Transactions on Engineering Management*, EM31 (November), pp. 154-161.

Cotgrove, S., & Box, S. (1970). *Science, industry, and society: Studies in the sociology of science*. London: George Allen & Unwin.

Dansereau, F., Graen, G., & Haga, W. (1975). A vertical dyad linkage approach to leadership within formal organizations: A longitudinal investigation of the role-making process. *Organizational Behavior and Human Performance*, Vol. 13, pp. 46-78.

Drucker, P.F. (1969). Managements' new role. *Harvard Business Review*. Vol. 47, pp. 49-54.

Dunegan, K., Tierney, P., & Duchon, D. (1992). Toward an understanding of innovative climate: Explaining variance in perceptions by divisional affiliation, work group interactions, and subordinate-manager exchanges. *IEEE Transactions on Engineering Management*, Vol. 39, pp. 227-236.

Eden, D. (1984). Self-fulfilling prophesy as a management tool: Harnessing Pygmalion. *Academy of Management Review*, Vol. 91, pp. 64-73.

Fast, N.D. (1979). The future of industrial new venture departments. *Industrial Marketing Management*, Vol. 8 (November), pp. 264-273.

Foxall, Gordon R. & Payne, Adrin F. (1989). Adaptors and innovators in Organizations: A Cross-Cultural Study of the Cognitive Styles of Managerial Functions and Subfunctions. *Human Relations*, Vol. 42, No. 7, pp. 639-649.

Graen, G., Cashman, J. (1975). A role-making model of leadership in formal organizations: A developmental approach. In J. Hunt & L. Larson (Eds.), *Leadership frontiers*, pp. 309-357.

Graen, G., & Novak, M., & Sommerkamp, P. (1982). The effects of leader-member exchange and job design on productivity and job satisfaction: Testing a dual attachment model. *Organizational Behavior and Human Performance*, Vol. 30, pp. 109-131.

Graen, G., & Scandura, T. (1987). Toward a psychology of dyadic organizing. In L. L. Cummings & B. M. Staw (Eds.). *Research in organizational behavior*, Vol. 9, pp. 175-208. Greenwich, CT: JAI Press.

Hair, J.F., Anderson, R.E., Tatham, R.L., & Black, W.C. (1992). *Multivariate Data Analysis with Readings*. New York: Macmillan.

Hayward, George, & Everett, Chris. (1983). Adaptors and innovators: Data from the Kirton Adaption-Innovation Inventory in a local authority setting. *Journal of Occupational Psychology*, Vol. 56, pp. 339-342.

Isaksen, S. (1987). An orientation to the frontiers of creativity research. In S. Isaksen (Ed.), *Frontiers of creativity research: Beyond the basics*. Buffalo, NY: Bearly Limited.

Jabri, M. (1991). The development of conceptually independent subscales in the measurement of modes of problem solving. *Educational and Psychological Measurement*, Vol. 51, pp. 975-983.

James, L., Hater, J., Gent, M., & Jones, A. (1977). Psychological climate: Implications from cognitive social learning theory and interactional psychology. *Personnel Psychology*, Vol. 31, pp. 783-813.

James, L., Hartman, E., Stebbins, M., & Jones, A. (1977). An examination of the relationship between psychological climate and a VIE model for work motivation. *Personnel Psychology*, Vol. 30, pp. 229-254.

James, L., James, L., & Ashe, D. (1990). The meaning of organizations: The role of cognition and values. In B. Schneider (Ed.), *Organizational climate and culture*, pp. 40-84. San Francisco: Jossey-Bass.

James, L., & Sells, S. (1981). Psychological climate: Theoretical perspectives and empirical research. In D. Magnussen (Ed.), *Toward a psychology of situations: An interfactional perspective*, pp. 275-295. Hillsdale, NJ: Erlbaum.

Kanter, R. (1983). *The change masters*. New York: Simon & Schuster.

Kanter, R. (1988). When a thousand flowers bloom: Structural, collective, and social conditions for innovation in organizations. In B.M. Staw & L.L. Cummings (Eds.), *Research in organizational behavior*, Vol 10, pp. 169-211. Greenwich, CT: JAI Press.

Kimberly, J.R. (1981). Managerial innoations. In W.H. Starbuck (Ed.), *Handbook of organizational design*, (Vol. 1, pp. 84-104). New York: Oxford University Press.

Kirton, Michael J. (1976). Adaptors and Innovators: A description and measure. *Journal of Applied Psychology*, Vol. 61, pp. 622-629.

Kirton, Michael J, (1984). Adaptors and innovators—Why new initiatives get blocked. *Long Range Planning*, Vol. 17, pp. 137-143.

Kirton, Michael J, (1987). *KAI manual* (2nd ed.). Hatfield, UK: Occupational Research Center.

Kirton, Michael J. (1994). *Adaptors and innovators: Styles of creativity and problem-solving*. London: Routledge.

Kirton, M.J., & Pender, S. (1982). The Adaption-Innovation Continuum, Occupational Type, and Course Selection. *Psychological Reports*, Vol. 51, pp. 883-886.

Koestler, A. (1964). *The act of creation*. London: Hutchinson.

Kozlowski, S., & Doherty, M. (1989). Integration of climate and leadership: Examination of a neglected topic. *Journal of Applied Psychology*, Vol. 74, pp. 546-553.

Livingston, J. (1969). Pygmalion in management. *Harvard Business Review*, Vol. 47, pp. 81-89.

Maidique, M.A. (1980). Entrepreneurs, champions, and technological innovation. *Sloan Management Review*, Vol. 21 (Winter), pp. 59-76.

Merton, R.K. (Ed.) (1957). *Bureaucratic structure and personality in social theory and social structure*. New York: Free Press of Glencoe.

Messick, S. (1976). *Individuality in learning: Implications of cognitive styles and creativity for human development*. San Francisco: Jossey-Bass.

Morrison, Philip, & Morrison, Emily (Eds.). (1961). *Charles Babbage on the principles and development of the calculator*. Mineola, NY: Dover Publications.

Mumford, M.C., & Gustafson, S.B. (1988). Creativity syndrome: Integration, application and innovation. *Psychological Bulletin*, 103, pp. 27-43.

Paolillo, J.G., & Brown, W.B. (1978). How organizational factors affect R&D innovation. *Research Management*, 21, pp. 12-15.

Pelz, D., & Andrews, F. (1966). Autonomy, coordination, and stimulation in relation to scientific achievement. *Behavioral Science*, Vol. 11, pp. 89-97.

Pritchard, R., & Karasick, B. (1973). The effects of organizational climate on managerial job performance and satisfaction. *Organizational Behavior and Human Performance*, Vol. 9, pp. 126-146.

Quinn, J.B. (1979). Techonological innovation, entrepreneurship and strategy. *Sloan Management Review*, Vol. 20 (Spring), pp. 19-30.

Rogers, C.R. (1959). Towards a theory of creativity. In H.H. Anderson (Ed.), *Creativity and its cultivation*, New York: Harper.

Schneider, B., & Reichers, A. (1983). On the etiology of climates. *Personnel Psychology*, Vol. 36, pp. 19-39.

Schoen, D.R. (1960). Managing technological innovation. *Harvard Business Review*, May-June, pp. 156-158.

Schroeder, R., Van de Ven, A., Scudder, G., & Polley, D. (1989). The development of innovation ideas. In A. Van de Ven, H. Angle, & M. Poole (Eds.), *Research on the management of innovation: The Minnesota studies*, pp. 107-134. New York: Harper & Row.

Scott, Susanne G., & Bruce, Reginald A., (June, 1994). Determinants of innovative behavior: a path model of individual innovation in the workplace. *Academy of Management Journal*, Vol. 37, No. 3, pp. 580-607.

Siegel, S., & Kaemmerer, W. (1978). Measuring the perceived support for innovation in organizations. *Journal of Applied Psychology*, Vol. 63, pp. 553-562.

Taylor, C. (1963). Variables related to creativity and productivity in men in two research laboratories. In C. Taylor & R. Barron (Eds.), *Scientific creativity: Its recognition and development*, pp. 513-597. New York: Wiley.

Tierney, Pamela. (1992). The contribution of leadership, supportive environment, and individual attributes to creative performance: A quantitative field study. (Doctoral dissertation, University of Cincinnati, 1992). *University Microfilms International*, Order Number 9313826.

Van de Ven, A. (1986). Central problems in the management of innovation. *Management Science*, Vol. 32, pp. 590-607.

Waldman, D., & Bass, B., (1991). Transformational leadership at different phases of the innovation process. *Journal of High Technology Management Research*, Vol. 2, pp. 169-180.

Weber, M. (1970). In H.H. Gerth & C.W. Mills (Eds. & Trans.) *From Max Weber: Essays in sociology*. London: Routledge and Kegan Paul.

West, M., & Farr, J. (1989). Innovation at work: Psychological perspectives. *Social Behavior*, Vol. 4, pp. 15-30.

West, M., & Farr, J. (1990). Innovation at work. In M. West & J. Farr (Eds.), *Innovation and creativity at work: Psychological and organizational strategies*. pp. 3-13. New York: Wiley.

Woodman, Richard W., Sawyer, John E., & Griffin, Ricky W. (April 1993). Toward a theory of organizational creativity. *The Academy of Management Review*, Vol. 18, No. 2, pp. 293-321.

Wren, Daniel A. (1994). *The evolution of management thought*. New York: Wiley.

Index